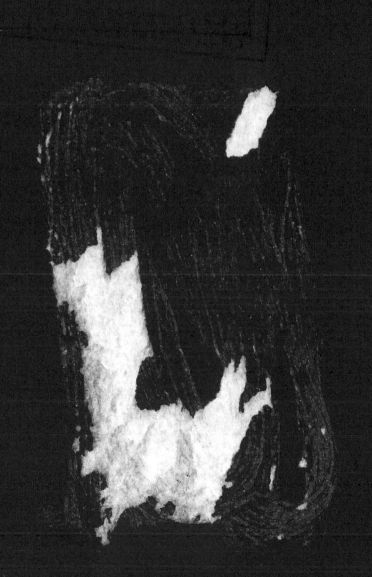

Teaching Basic
JUMPING

Teaching Basic
JUMPING

MARTIN DIGGLE

J. A. ALLEN · LONDON

British Library Cataloguing in Publication Data
A catalogue record for this book is available from the British Library

ISBN 0–85131–706–5
First published in 1990 by J. A. Allen & Co Ltd
Revised edition 2000
Reprinted 2003

Published in Great Britain by
J. A. Allen
Clerkenwell House, 45-47 Clerkenwell Green,
London, EC1R 0HT

Design by Paul Saunders
Photographs by Vanessa Britton
Illustrations by Rodney Paull
Cartoons by Ann Pilgrim
Front cover illustrations by Maggie Raynor

Typesetting by Textype Cambridge
Colour separation by Tenon & Polert Colour Scanning Ltd
Printed in China by Midas Printing International Ltd.

The teaching and learning of riding is not quite so easy as it sounds, I'm afraid. Many good riders, and even some people who are considered good teachers, are limited in their ability to evaluate accurately another rider's performance because they have lost the capacity to really see what is there; instead, they only see what they want to see. So it is a common experience to find a performance praised because some detail of it that is particularly important to the observer has been performed in accordance with the dogma he espouses...

The best teacher of all, if you examine his instructions carefully enough, is no writer, no instructor, no other rider – it is the horse you are riding, and his performance will always be the soundest criterion of all the appropriateness and 'correctness' of your actions.

WILLIAM STEINKRAUS *Riding and Jumping*

CONTENTS

List of photographs

PREFACE

AS OUR MEMBERS know, the Association of British Riding Schools is the only professional organisation involved with riding schools. As such, we are delighted to be presenting this book in association with J. A. Allen.

Teaching Basic Jumping will be the first in a series of books which we hope will be helpful not only to our members but also to individuals outside the association who have a genuine desire to improve their knowledge and teaching ability – they, I hope will be the ABRS members of tomorrow!

Feedback is an essential part of getting the product right. We would greatly welcome your input, not only about the content of this book, but also about the subject matter and content of future titles in the series. Remember that these are books for you, for your employees, for your students. If we are to produce the books you want, we have to know what books you need.

I feel sure I speak for everyone when I say that through books like these we have an opportunity to further our aim of improving teaching methods and promoting a better understanding of pupil/teacher psychology, never forgetting that none of this would be possible without the willing co-operation of the most vital and valued member of our profession – the horse.

PAULINE HARRIS, CHAIRMAN ABRS

FOREWORD

THIS IS A welcome publication detailing the basic principles of jumping and in my firm opinion is essential reading for all equestrians who include jumping in their 'equestrian vocabulary'.

With these basic principles simply explained – yet detailed and quite thorough – not only will the pupils of riding teachers further their enjoyment and fun in tackling all types of obstacles from poles on the ground to cross-country fences, but their active participation in jumping under all types of conditions will be safer for both horse and rider.

I have read hundreds of books written on the science and art of jumping. Few are written in such simple, concise, and straightforward equestrian terminology.

This is quite a unique book on jumping, as we are given in their correct order and sequence, learned comment on:

The Qualities of the Teacher…

The Pupil's Background…

Preliminary Explanations… etc. etc.

so that everyone – even the most nervous rider – is likely to enhance their confidence with a teacher familiar with the Author's theoretical and practical experience and applications.

Seldom are we offered from authors and publishers – as a team – such a well-explained guide on the most essential of equestrian matters, i.e. correctly detailed basic principles, laying an excellent foundation for an aspect of horsemanship which appears to be totally confused with muddled misinformation. This small book is based on sound, practical common-sense, enhanced and enriched by equestrian scholarship.

For those interested in horsemanship – and jumping in particular – the riding teacher, the pupil, and the general rider will find much to increase the potential of their horse(s) and greatly add more pleasure and safety to their jumping whether indoors or outdoors.

CHARLES HARRIS FBHS FABRS

INTRODUCTION

THE MAIN concern of this book is the introduction of novice riders to a safe and effective jumping technique. It is not my intention to suggest to experienced trainers how to refine the skills of advanced pupils, nor would I presume to do so.

It is, however, self-evident that pupils are unlikely to become advanced – or anything like it – unless their introduction to jumping is such that they first develop confidence and effectiveness over small obstacles. Were it the case that a substantial majority of riders progressed along such lines, then there would be little point in writing this book. Unfortunately, extensive observation suggests that this is not the case; a disquieting proportion of novice riders do not progress to the stage at which they have the confidence or ability to tackle even a small course of jumps with success.

In any field of learning, it seems inevitable that a small proportion of pupils will show extraordinary aptitude, and a further proportion will, for various reasons, experience an abnormal degree of difficulty. However, in cases where a significant number of pupils fail to make satisfactory progress, one obvious area for investigation is the standard of tuition received, together with the philosophy and principles upon which that tuition is based.

In saying this, I am not, for a moment, suggesting that all jumping problems are the fault of the instructor, or that all instructors are teaching incorrectly. I am, however, convinced that, *too often*, confused and ineffective riding over jumps (with the risk this entails) *is* a direct consequence of tuition received. This claim is not made merely because jumping is often taught in a manner with which I disagree, but as a result of observing the effects of such teaching, and of numerous conversations with its victims. Much of this experience has been with keen, intelligent adult riders, who have repeatedly experienced practical difficulties, and have expressed confusion and loss of confidence, sometimes to the extent of having real disquiet about jumping at all. It seems a great pity that this state of affairs should exist, not only because of possible reflections upon the general standard of tuition, but also because it effectively debarrs many riders from enjoying those branches of equitation which can be most exhilarating.

My purpose, therefore, is to intercede on behalf of novice pupils, to ask instructors to examine their own theories and practices, and to abandon any tendencies toward mystique, muddled thinking, erroneous or unsafe instruction. The acid test of any teacher's ability is how their pupils perform in isolation (that is, how much they have actually *learnt*). Bearing this in mind, there are two basic questions which jumping instructors should ask of themselves: 'do my pupils come back from the local show with rosettes, or with muddy breeches and tales of woe?' and, more fundamentally, 'do my pupils have the confidence and enthusiasm to *go* to the local show?'.

CHAPTER 1

QUALITIES OF THE TEACHER

THE QUALITIES which make a good teacher (in any sphere) can be broadly categorised as:

1. Sound theoretical understanding.

2. A degree of practical experience appropriate to the level at which tuition is offered.

3. Having the pupil's interests at heart.

4. The ability to communicate effectively.

Let us examine these factors in the context of giving instruction in riding over jumps.

Theoretical Understanding

If a pupil is really to *learn* about any subject, it is of fundamental importance that he gains a proper grasp of the underlying principles. This will provide him with a firm foundation from which to build up his store of knowledge and technical skills. Being told 'do this', 'do that' is not, by itself, sufficient; even if everything the pupil is told is correct, such isolated snippets of information will leave him guessing at the connections between them.

Therefore, although it is often necessary to give concise instruction on a specific point, the teacher must, at an appropriate moment, be able and willing to explain such instructions in an overall context. More important still, he must avoid subjecting pupils to a regime of glib generalisations and 'catch-all' phrases, which do not educate, but leave pupils in a welter of half-truths, contradictions and confusion.

In order to avoid such pitfalls, it is necessary for the jumping instructor to understand the basic principles of riding on the flat, the equine mechanics (and, as far as possible, psychology) of jumping, and to appreciate how, why, in what circumstances and to what degree the horse may vary his jumping action from what might be described as the 'norm'. He must also understand what the rider should do in both normal and abnormal circumstances, and when, how much, and to what extent the rider should seek to influence the factors surrounding the act of jumping. This brings us to the next attribute of the teacher.

Practical Experience

The cynical old saying 'those who can, do – those who can't, teach' may, in some cases, be true, but that is not to say that such a state of affairs is desirable, or even acceptable. Although it is often true that the best teachers are not the very best practitioners (and vice versa), it is fair to say that the best teachers invariably demonstrate (or have demonstrated) the ability to perform to a highly proficient standard. This is hardly surprising, since the links between theoretical understanding and practical experience are very strong. However, it is important to understand that these links involve more than a simple 'one way' process of putting theory into practice. The wise practitioner will temper, refine and adapt his theory in the light of his experiences, and it is this process which makes experience such a desirable quality in the teacher.

This is not to say that untested theory is necessarily wrong, simply that it is untested. It may be useful to examine this point in more detail, in the hope that those who have actually done relatively little jumping may be dissuaded from devaluing their instruction with the dogma of inexperience.

There is an unfortunate tendency (not confined to riders) to consider pure theory in the same light as the theorems of geometry. The crux of a theorem is that it is demonstrably true for any and all cases, but this is only possible because it relates to a figure which is strictly limited by its own definition (for example, *any* circle is a perfectly round two-dimensional figure; all physical differences between circles are directly related to differences between their radii). Such narrow limitations do not pertain to most areas of practical activity; certainly not to riding over jumps. Here, there are many variable factors, the possible permutations of which are practically endless. Common sense suggests that it is unrealistic to try to deal with so many variables by the rigid application of a few supposedly inviolate rules. Intelligent theorising does not work like that; it is, rather, a system of reasoning to account for that which has been perceived or conceived. In order that it can do so, it must not be dismissive; where faithfully-reproduced theory does not work in practice, the reason must be established and the theory revised accordingly. The old line about 'the exception that proves the rule' will not wash – it is nothing more than self-admitted nonsense.

It is important to emphasize that we are talking about *revising* theory; practical failure does not necessarily mean that a whole concept is wrong and should be abandoned in favour of its antithesis. To give a practical example, it may be that a rider tackles a large, untrimmed hedge strictly in accordance with his theoretical assessment of all known factors, and suffers a fall because of a concealed ditch on the landing side. Had the ditch not existed, the jump would probably have been successful. Therefore, where he *knows* that there is no concealed obstacle, the rider will not need to adjust his theory or practice at similar hedges in the future. The theory has, however, proved inadequate as a formula for jumping each and every hedge, and will therefore have to be expanded. Merely *altering* the theory – asking the horse for greater speed and effort at every hedge in case there is a ditch on the far side – would be unsatisfactory on several counts; it would often be unnecessary, it would sometimes be impractical or impossible and, in some circumstances (for instance if the landing side were significantly higher than the take-off) it might increase the likelihood of a further fall. Thus it will become apparent to the intelligent rider that he cannot successfully adopt *any* pre-determined technique at every hedge he faces, because all may not be as it seems. This may trigger a train of thought which entertains not only the possibility of ditches, but of concealed hazards (wire, huge drops, farm machinery, etc.) in general. As a result, the rider may determine that it is a good principle either to check unfamiliar obstacles before jumping them, or to follow someone who has local knowledge. The first course will give him a clear picture, and the second a general idea, of what is required, and he can do whatever is appropriate, rather than pull a rigid theory 'out of the hat' and apply it in the spirit of blind hope.

Elasticity of thought is not, of course, relevant only in a cross-country environment; it is of equal value in the teaching arena. Unfortunately, it is often noticeable by its absence, a prime example being concentration upon symptoms of errors rather than their root causes. At a more subtle level, the idea of things not always being what they seem should be continually borne in mind, especially when dealing with problems originating in the horse. While an instructor is observing a horse, and the pupil is riding, it is obvious that neither is doing both. What is often less obvious – though equally true – is that *neither* is in possession of all the available information; the pupil having a very limited view of the horse, and the instructor having no actual 'feel' of it at all. Certainly, any competent teacher should have an educated idea of what is wrong and why, but, since his perception is incomplete, his analysis may not be entirely accurate, and this will detract from the value of his advice. This is one instance where it may prove advantageous for the instructor to ride the horse, and thus represents an example of the immediate benefit of practical experience.

In such a situation, the instructor's *background* experience is also important. Whether his initial impression of the horse is wholly confirmed or not, he must demonstrate the practical ability to improve its performance. The main reason for this is, of course, purely instructional; the teacher showing the pupil what to do. It is undeniable, however, that a successful demonstration is likely to enhance the pupil's respect for the teacher – with the practical bonus that he may take greater heed of future advice. If, on the other hand, the instructor is unwilling – or unable(!) – to give such a demonstration, then he should be hardly surprised if the respect of his pupils tends to wane. (Further to this point, my own observation has been that it is quite common for instructors to ride pupils' horses during lessons on the flat; it is, however, rare for them to do so during jumping lessons. I leave readers to form their own opinions on this matter.)

Up until now, we have concentrated upon the capacity of experience to indicate error or inadequacy in theory, but it plays an equally valuable role when it reinforces or confirms theory. Indeed, the acknowledged principles of equitation could be said to derive from theories which have proved repeatedly effective when practised by many different riders in many different circumstances. However, whether the instructor is extolling a personal theory or an acknowledged principle, he will do so with greater conviction if he *knows*, rather than just believes, that it works.

The converse of this is also true: the instructor will take greater pains to point out and correct an error if he has personal experience of its effects. This is not to imply that instructors do or should make errors habitually, but everyone makes mistakes sometimes – the trick is to turn them to one's advantage by learning from them. Thus even a negative experience can be of value to the teacher; firstly, because he can learn from it himself, secondly, because it may help him identify more readily with his pupils' problems, and thirdly because it may remind him to encourage pupils to analyse and learn from their own errors.

Experience is, then, an important quality of the teacher, and this brings us to the question of what actual experience is appropriate to one who gives instruction in basic jumping. In general terms, it can be said that the practical experience should be such as will reinforce the theoretical understanding required. This will entail having ridden a variety of horses in different stages of training over a variety of obstacles, in different circumstances and terrain – in other words, the experience should be as broad-based as possible. It is important to recognise that a wide grounding – even at a fairly modest level – is of more value to the teacher than a narrow range of experience at a more exalted level.

To give a practical illustration from the competitive sphere, it is likely that a rider who has ridden a number of moderate horses with modest but consistent success will be better prepared to instruct than one whose whole experience consists of competing at a higher level on a talented 'schoolmaster'. This is not to say that there is no value in the latter course, nor to denigrate the teaching potential of successful competition riders *per se*. It is just that, if not balanced by other experiences, such a background can provide a false perspective, and put the individual out of touch with the realities facing novice riders on less able horses.

To pursue this point of dealing with reality, I would suggest that anyone whose sole experience of jumping consists of riding well-trained horses in a 'benign' environment has insufficient experience to teach novice jumping. This may seem a harsh judgement, the counter-argument being that novice pupils should, themselves, be riding well-trained horses in a similar environment. This, in principle, is perfectly true in the early stages, but it is far from certain that it will always happen in practice. Furthermore, assuming that the instruction is such that the pupils progress, it will not be long before some of them will wish to ride in less ordered circumstances (trying more demanding horses, attempting first cross-country obstacles, entering minor competitions etc.) . At this juncture, they will certainly need a teacher who can guide them by virtue of his personal experience, rather than misguide them with misapplied or inappropriate theory.

Having the Pupils' Interests at Heart

It is an inherent quality of a good teacher that he genuinely wants his pupils to improve, and takes pleasure in their doing so. He will also be sympathetic towards their problems, but in a practical, positive way. A good teacher does not say 'never mind' in isolation; he takes pains to establish the cause of a difficulty and effect a cure – or, at least, an improvement.

It is part of a good teacher's philosophy that he seek to *educate*; that is, he imparts solid, reliable information and encourages his pupils to understand and absorb it. To this end, he will make it plain that he welcomes questions, and even plainer that he *expects* his pupils to require further explanation of anything they do not understand. Within the framework of a riding lesson, such an approach requires occasional periods of rest, during which principles can be discussed and questions answered. At such times, all pupils should be encouraged to listen to all points, not just those which they feel pertinent to their own current circumstances. This procedure does not mean, however, that queries which require urgent consideration should be 'put off' until the next convenient break – especially if they involve matters of safety.

With regard to safety, riding (in any form) is a sport in which having the pupils' interests at heart must include concern for their physical welfare. Obviously, this means paying attention to standard safety matters (clothing, tack, horses, commonsense procedures, knowing what to do in the event of an accident, etc.), but the instructor should also be careful that his actual *teaching* is as safe as possible. Although, of course, it is not possible to guarantee that pupils will always do exactly as they are told it should be self-evident that, when they do so, they should not thereby injure or imperil themselves. In this respect, it should be remembered that pupils are not 'guinea pigs' supplied to test (and be blamed for the failure of) the instructor's pet theories!

The Ability to Communicate Effectively

Regardless of their level of understanding and experience, no one will be a good teacher unless they can communicate effectively. The ability to communicate *really* well can, perhaps, be considered a gift, but anyone can improve their 'natural' level of ability by giving some thought to what communication entails. For the teacher, the crux of communication is to convey information precisely and memorably; it will be apparent that just speaking sufficiently loudly and clearly – though essential – will not fulfil these criteria.

Precise communication entails telling pupils *exactly* what they should do, for example 'fold the upper body forward from the hips', rather than 'lean forwards'. It may sometimes be legitimate to abbreviate more familiar instructions, *but only once it is clear that all pupils understand fully the implications* — instructors should never *assume* that their own 'verbal shorthand' will be understood. Precision in communication will be abetted by giving positive rather than negative instructions whenever possible. This is simply because the former are inherently more precise, 'do this' being definite while 'don't do that' leaves the way open for a number of alternative actions.

The ability to communicate precisely stems largely from clarity of thought which, in turn, is greatly aided by a sound knowledge and understanding of the subject. It is apparent, therefore, that there must be an inter-relationship between the teacher's attributes; he must have the ability to communicate his knowledge, but he also *requires* the knowledge to enhance his ability to communicate.

The ability to communicate memorably is rooted in two basic factors, which might be described as the 'scientific' and the 'artistic'.

The 'science' of memorable communication is based on the premise that a pupil is most likely to remember advice or instruction if he understands the underlying reasons for its being given, and thereby appreciates its significance. Therefore, in addition to giving precise instructions, the teacher should also give clear explanations; he should avoid instructing in a string of glib cliches, which carry the risk of being dismissed by the pupils as insignificant fads.

The 'artistic' side of communication is manifest mainly in those people for whom communication is a 'gift'. It can be of great value if attributes such as humour, imagination and mimicry are used constructively to impress information on the minds of the recipients. However, it is essential that anyone pursuing such a course has both a genuine attribute and a sound knowledge of their subject. Using 'the gift of the gab' to cover up flawed understanding is not effective teaching, and forced attempts at humour, etc., will merely prove embarrassing and distracting.

This brings us to consideration of the instructor's manner. The relationship and empathy between parties is an important element in communication, and the instructor should always bear this in mind. While it is probable that a keen, intelligent pupil will take great pains to listen to anyone whose knowledge and ability he respects, it is undoubtedly true that he will be greatly assisted if they are easy to listen to and understand. Where less committed pupils are concerned, it is likely that *unless* the teacher possesses these attributes, he will fail to 'get through' to any extent, regardless of his other qualities.

It is difficult to define exactly what makes somebody easy to listen to, but it is certain that interesting and pleasant tones are two of the main factors. These may be promoted if the instructor thinks of his role as one of giving friendly help and advice. This is not to imply that he should be fawning and ingratiating, nor that he should not criticize (constructively) where criticism is due; it is simply that thinking in such terms may help him adopt a more natural attitude toward his pupils, and thus communicate with them as one interested party to another. Such an approach is likely to be more helpful to both parties than a starchy, formal manner. This latter can easily alienate pupils, making them feel as though they are being drilled or processed, and it often has the effect of engendering in the instructor the faults of monotony, pointless repetition and glibness.

A natural, conversational style can help pupils not only to listen, but also to understand what they hear. In normal conversation, sensitive, intelligent people will adapt their manner of speech in accordance with the individuals to whom they are speaking. This is not – or should not be – a question of deference or condescension, but simply an attempt to communicate to optimum effect; to 'speak the other person's language'. As such, it remains relevant within the field of teaching. If instructing a cross-section of pupils of differing ages, temperaments, background, etc., it will be apparent that the use of exactly the same language, phraseology, analogies, etc., will not be of equal value to each. Although the teacher should not compromise the content or quality of his instruction, nor use incorrect *equestrian* terminology ('pull the reins', etc.), he should endeavour to couch the instruction in terms which he believes will be most readily understood. This is best achieved by remembering that pupils are individuals, and treating them as such.

CHAPTER 2

THE PUPILS' BACKGROUND

IT IS OF GREAT help to any teacher to know something of the background, influences, preliminary attitudes and preparedness of his pupils. These factors will obviously vary from person to person, and it is important to avoid forming some generalised opinion about 'the' pupil. Nevertheless, there is value in considering, in general terms, those influences which may play a part in moulding the thinking and riding of novice pupils.

Since jumping is simply one branch of equitation, it follows that a rider's general equestrian background will have an initial influence upon his approach to jumping. These days, an increasingly high proportion of people start to ride when adult, and an increasing proportion of all beginners come from a 'non-horsy' background. The nett result is that, although perhaps more riders who start jumping now have a 'formal' grounding on the flat, fewer have the more traditional background of gymkhanas, mounted games, etc., which in the past, helped promote balance, confidence, and what might be described as a 'hot-blooded' enjoyment of riding. In consequence, many pupils will look on anything other than basic school work and fairly sedate hacking as totally different activities, and such conceptions can and do colour attitudes towards jumping.

This situation is compounded, in many cases, by the individual's own observation of jumping. It is by no means unusual for this to consist almost entirely of watching major competitions on television, with the result that 'jumping' is perceived as a very formidable undertaking. A further complication is that keen observers will almost inevitably start formulating their own ideas about technique – an admirable trait, but one which carries the risk that they may start riding over jumps with various misconceptions already entrenched.

However, despite influences which may be misleading and unhelpful, the majority of reasonably keen riders reach a stage at which they want to 'have a go' at jumping. This is probably because it is one of the most obviously exciting-looking aspects of equestrian sport, and appeals to the general desire for challenge and achievement which exists in everyone to some degree. This does not mean, however, that everyone will approach the prospect of jumping with the same attitude, and the instructor may have to contend with everything from timid trepidation to blatant over-eagerness. Furthermore, such attitudes may relate neither to the pupil's actual riding ability, nor to his general temperament and personality. Although an interesting comment upon human nature, such disparities do not make the instructor's task any easier.

Nevertheless, provided that he is dealing with pupils who are basically reasonable and realistic people, the instructor should be able to overcome any difficulties arising from their various attitudes; indeed, it is an integral part of his job to do so. Interestingly, in many cases, it may prove more straightforward to deal with the initially diffident than with the over-eager. Given sound instruction and gentle encouragement, the former should gain confidence as their skill and experience increase – a natural progression. With the latter, there is the need for a more complex process of curbing impatience and over-confidence without dampening natural enthusiasm – a situation which calls for a measure of diplomacy.

The instructor's really serious problem occurs when he is confronted with pupils who are not yet sufficiently proficient on the flat to begin jumping. The preliminary level of proficiency can be defined, in general terms, as an ability to exercise a fair degree of control at walk, trot and canter – a definition which should encompass an absence of serious postural defects (those which habitually affect balance and rein contact). It is a considerable advantage (though not necessarily a requirement) for pupils to have some experience of riding in the open at canter, with slightly shortened stirrups and a modified posture. No one, whatever their attitude, can be expected to ride over jumps successfully without first having such a grounding on the flat, and, when a lack of this grounding is linked to the more extreme attitudes of timidity or audacity, it becomes a recipe for disaster.

In theory, the solution to lack of pupil experience is simple: if a pupil is not yet capable, he should not be encouraged or allowed to start jumping. Common sense suggests that this solution should be inviolate; in practice, however, it is not always an easy stance to adopt. The instructor who should have least difficulty in this respect is the freelance teacher of private pupils.

No one can ride over jumps successfully without first having a grounding on the flat.

In the first instance, he is likely to have built up a rapport with his clients, who will therefore trust his judgement. Secondly, it is unlikely that – in the absence of external pressures – any pupil who is diffident about jumping will be in an undue hurry to start too early (although, with younger pupils, there is the possibility of interference from pushy parents). If he is confronted by over-eager pupils (or their families), the private instructor has the time and opportunity to discuss the situation in detail, and explain fully the need for competence on the flat. He may, indeed, be able to give the pupil added incentive to improve his flatwork by stressing the significance of various factors (impulsion, contact, accuracy etc.) in the context of riding over jumps. The instructor operating on a one-to-one basis also has the advantage that there is no risk of complications arising from a pupil's concern about 'loss of face' among classmates if told he is not yet ready to start jumping.

This problem is, however, just one of those which may confront the instructor of class lessons at a commercial establishment – and the less influence he has upon the organisation of lessons, the more prevalent the problems may be. If the programming of lessons is too 'automatic', pupils may be railroaded into jumping too early; this can occur if new pupils are slotted into a class which is not really suitable, or simply as a result of differing speeds of progress. Also, some stables seem to have a general policy of introducing all pupils to jumping too soon, and others appear too ready to bow to pressure from over-eager clients.

These various procedures create circumstances unsatisfactory for pupil and teacher alike. If all, or most, of the pupils are not yet capable, then attempting a class jumping lesson is basically a waste of everybody's time, and is also potentially hazardous. If abilities are too varied, it will be difficult for the instructor to give a cohesive, flowing lesson; he can hardly pitch the lesson mainly at the more able pupils for fear of endangering and embarrassing the less able, and, if he pitches it mainly at the latter, the former may become bored, impatient and inattentive – states of mind which may impair safety.

An astute and experienced instructor who has to 'make the best' of such circumstances will probably cope passably well, but the fact remains that he is saddled with an unfair task, and it will be extremely difficult for him to ensure that each pupil gets full value from the lesson. In a similar situation, a less experienced instructor is likely to have a real struggle, and may even make errors of judgement which contribute towards an accident.

Thus we may conclude that the problem of trying to teach jumping before pupils are ready is not one which can be satisfactorily solved, and it should therefore be avoided. This, ultimately, is the responsibility of the stable manager/proprietor. Whilst not belittling the pressures and constraints under which many stables operate, I suggest that the preparedness of pupils should *always* be the major factor in determining policy regarding jumping lessons. Although this may contribute to occasional complications, these will be far outweighed by overall benefits to instructors, horses, clients and the reputation of the stable.

CHAPTER 3

FACILITIES, HORSES AND EQUIPMENT

HAVING LOOKED at the pre-requisites of teacher and pupil, we should now consider those elements which represent the 'classroom' and learning resources.

The Teaching Area

Early jumping lessons should take place in a properly enclosed arena, whose walls/boundary fence are in good repair (no splintered kicking boards or rails, no protruding nails, etc.). The arena surface should be level, with suitable footing; it should not be too firm or too deep and 'holding', and it should be free from false (slippery or boggy) patches.

In size, the arena should be no smaller than the standard 40 x 20 metres; anything less will be too restricting, especially for group lessons. A somewhat larger arena will provide greater scope for jump placement. In particular, greater width will facilitate early attempts to approach jumps on the centre line; a useful placement for the instructor, but rather demanding for novice pupils in a standard arena. While a jumping lesson is in progress, it is undesirable for the teaching area to be used for any other purposes (schooling, lungeing, other lessons) even if it is extensive. Such activities can prove a dangerous distraction for both horses and riders, and may possibly cause a collision.

Jump-building Materials

All materials used in the construction of jumps should be robust and well-maintained, with jump poles being at least 10 cm (4 in) in diameter. In the early stages, it will assist pupils if all jumps have proper wings (or one wing

Early jumping lessons should take place in a properly enclosed area.

and the arena perimeter), and any superfluous jump cups should be removed and stored in a safe place – not left to become half-buried in the floor of the arena. Jump cups should be secured to wings by blunt-ended pins (preferably of the captive type); six-inch nails are *not* a suitable substitute!

Cavalletti are useful items of equipment, but they should not be stacked pyramid-fashion to build jumps. If hit, such jumps tend to roll forwards rather than fall, and can thus bring a horse down.

Horses

Finding horses who come near to being the ideal 'novice ride' is never easy, and does not become any easier in the context of jumping. The type required is obedient, tolerant, honest and a clever and careful jumper; the sort who will do his best given anything other than total hindrance.

Since the number of horses who truly fulfil these criteria is limited, there may not always be enough to mount every rider in a class lesson. This means that other horses will have to be used, and these must be selected with care.

It should be self-evident that certain types of horse are *not* suitable for introducing novice riders to jumping, but observation suggests either that this is not always so, or that some stables are prepared to use them regardless. It may, therefore, be useful to examine these categories, and establish why they are unsuitable.

Unsound Horses

'Unsoundness' is a broad term, and even named conditions can cover a wide category of problems. It is quite true, for example, that some horses with conditions such as navicular, stringhalt and 'back trouble' can, and do, jump. Depending upon the precise nature and extent of the ailment, and the nature and circumstances of the jumping, this may or may not be morally acceptable, and may or may not represent an acceptable degree of risk to horse and *owner-rider*. As a general principle, however, it is both unwise and unacceptable to mount paying clients on horses known to be unsound, since the existence of the unsoundness inevitably poses a potential danger.

Consideration should also be given to the effects of more unusual infirmities/abnormalities. For instance, one-eyed horses are not that rare, and those who have lost an eye after being trained will often continue to jump happily and effectively. However, because of their affliction, they often prefer or need to approach fences somewhat crooked, a trait which can pose problems when trying to teach a pupil to ride a straight approach. Additionally, a psychological factor is involved in that it is inherently disconcerting for a rider about to begin jumping to be given a horse with only one eye. Thus, however honest a one-eyed horse may be, it is preferable not to use him for jumping lessons until pupils have reached a stage at which they can appreciate, and allow for, his infirmity.

Young and/or Inexperienced Horses

These tend to 'wander' into their fences, and jump unnecessarily 'big', and otherwise erratically. They are thus unsuitable for novice pupils who, in any case, should not be expected to perform the task of schooling.

Keen, Strong Horses

Horses who are strong and/or excitable rides, and tend to rush their fences, are, most definitely, not novice rides. An apprehensive rider will almost certainly 'hang on' to such a horse's head continually, producing bad results both on the flat and over jumps, and consequently losing confidence. A more intrepid but inexperienced rider will usually allow such a horse to get away

*...it is undesirable for the
teaching area to be used
for other purposes*

from him, to the extent that the horse speeds up until totally out of control. Even assuming that an accident does not occur immediately, the rider is likely to become used to being 'taken' into his fences, rather than learning to ride the approaches, and therefore risks being a future victim of a sudden and violent refusal or run-out.

It should be noted that simply fitting a more severe bit to such a horse *will not* convert him into a suitable mount for a novice jumper. The likely consequence of such action is that the horse will be punished in the mouth, become upset, and jump badly; a state of affairs unhelpful to both he and his rider.

Very Lazy Horses

It can be argued that there is virtue in teaching jumping on somewhat phlegmatic horses who do no more than they are asked, since pupils will learn the need to ride at jumps and give an aid at take-off. This is not to say, however, that there is any point or use in expecting a pupil to jump a horse who is so lazy and inactive that he might be mistaken for a log. Such a horse will require too much effort from a rider trying to absorb new ideas and techniques, and it is discouraging and demeaning for a pupil to expend a great deal of energy only to have his mount climb over a jump one leg at a time.

In addition to being of a suitable type, it is important that horses are individually suited to their riders in terms of size. This should be a simple matter of common sense, but it is one to which surprisingly little attention is given. It should be borne in mind that a small, short-legged rider is certain to be less effective on a large, wide horse than one of appropriate size and, when stirrup leathers have been shortened, a grossly over-horsed rider may feel both physically uncomfortable and insecure. A tall, long-legged rider *light* enough to ride a small horse/pony may find 'lack of front' disconcerting when starting jumping, and may also have problems with length of leathers. Difficulty in getting his lower legs 'on' the horse may cause him to shorten his leathers beyond his 'norm' whilst riding on the flat and, if he shortens them further for jumping (in response to an instruction given automatically) he may end up riding excessively short on too small a horse – a precarious combination for a novice.

While the points above are aimed primarily at those giving group instruction at a riding school, they remain relevant for the private tutor. The latter should bring any form of unsuitability tactfully to the notice of the owner-rider and, where possible, help achieve a remedy before embarking upon a course of jumping instruction.

Tack and Equipment

In any area of equestrian activity it is important that tack is both safe (of good quality and in good condition) and appropriate (suits and fits both horse and rider). Because of the extra activity and additional stresses involved, these criteria assume even greater importance when riding over jumps. Regardless of whether or not he is personally responsible for supplying and fitting tack, any instructor who has his pupils' interests at heart should pay attention to this issue, and it is sound practice to check each pupil's tack before starting a lesson. General points to remember are:

1. Dirty, damaged, ill-fitting or incorrectly adjusted tack will not only cause discomfort/injury to the horse, but will adversely affect his performance, possibly to the extent of placing the rider at risk.

2. If doubt exists as to the condition/state of repair of any item, it must be replaced *forthwith*. Since it is by no means unknown for damage to occur in reins, girths and stirrup leathers before any defect has become apparent, it is untenable to countenance the continued use of such items in which defects are obvious. There is little comfort to a prostrate rider in having the instructor murmur 'I thought that stitching needed seeing to'.

Matters to consider when assessing individual items of tack are:

1. **Bridle** should be properly adjusted and fastened.

2. **Bit** horses suitable for novice riders should go kindly in a straight-forward snaffle; this should be in good condition, of the right size, and correctly fitted.

3. **Reins** the fastening to the bit rings should be secure and in good condition. The buckle joining the reins should be in good condition but – especially when riders reach the stage of starting cross-country jumping – it is sensible for reins to be knotted at the buckle end. If reins are excessively long, and cannot be readily replaced, it is essential that they are knotted in this fashion to prevent loops hanging around the rider's feet. Reins which are unduly short should be avoided, firstly because they may have been mended too often, and secondly because they will not enable the rider to slip them if necessary. Reins should be clean, but not oiled to the extent that they are virtually impossible to hold. Very thin, 'bootlace' reins should not be used, being so insubstantial that riders feel they can only maintain contact by continually gripping them very firmly, thus 'deadening' their hands.

4. **Neckstrap** should be standard equipment on a horse jumped by a beginner. Most neckstraps are elderly stirrup leathers, but they should not be so elderly as to be unfit for their purpose.

5. **Martingale** if a running martingale is used, it should be correctly adjusted, and 'stops' should be properly positioned on the reins. (It may sound improbable, but I have seen a horse get a martingale ring caught round a tooth – and panic – as a result of incorrect adjustment and wrongly positioned 'stops'.)

6. **Saddle** It is obvious that the saddle should fit the horse, but it should also be neither much too large, nor too small, for the rider. It should be of either jumping or good general purpose design (initially, pupils may

feel more at home in the latter); it is unreasonable to expect novice riders to jump in a dressage or showing saddle, however well it may fit the horse!

The saddle must be in good condition; adequately stuffed and with a tree which is neither broken nor twisted. Attention should be given to the webbing and stitching linking girth tabs to tree, and to the tabs themselves; in particular, girth buckle holes should not be over-enlarged or splitting.

Safety catches on stirrup bars must be down.

7. **Girth** buckles, stitching and the girth itself must be in good condition, and the girth must be clean and correctly fitted. It should be of such length that, when adequately tight at the start of a lesson, the facility exists to tighten it at least two holes on each side (pupils should be reminded to check girths before jumping commences, and again after the first few jumps). Girths made of inherently stretchy material should be avoided; in this respect, it should be noted that freshly-washed lampwick can stretch appreciably in the space of a few minutes. As far as elasticated girths are concerned, I would not have one as a gift.

Unsuitable tack will adversely affect the performance of horse and rider

8. **Stirrup leathers** should receive similar attention as girths and girth tabs. Old, stretched leathers (noticeable by variations in thickness and width) and those with splits radiating from buckle holes should be replaced. Leathers must be of such length, and so punched, that they can be adjusted to suit the individual using them; the pupil should not have to ride at a length dictated by the leathers!

9. **Stirrup irons** must not be twisted or cracked. They should be neither so big that there is risk of the rider's feet passing right through them, nor so small that the rider's feet may become trapped. Heavy (steel) irons with rubber treads are ideal.

As far as the riders are concerned, their comfort and efficiency will be greatly increased if they are wearing proper riding boots and breeches/jodhpurs. Wellingtons, and similar boots, which are short in the calf, usually snag under the saddle flaps when stirrup leathers are shortened, while jeans, etc., ruck up around the knees and tend to constrict parts best left unconstricted. Riding gloves not only afford a better hold of the reins in wet weather, but may protect against grazes in the event of a fall.

With regard to protection, pupils should wear hard hats which conform to current British Safety standards. Both in view of recent litigation, and with regard to clients welfare, it would appear sensible for commercial establishments to insist upon this, and the old practice of hiring/loaning soft, fungoid hats of dubious origin should certainly be avoided.

Class Size

This is an important factor in the learning/teaching process. From the point of view of both pupil and teacher, the ideal number of pupils in a class is one. Obviously, it would be impractical for commercial schools to operate solely on the basis of individual lessons, but it *is* important to strike a reasonable compromise between commercial practicalities and the safety and value of tuition offered. A very good long-term reason for this is that failure to do so will result in loss of custom.

Specific reasons for not over-crowding lessons are:

1. Jumping lessons require more space than is necessary for lessons in flatwork. Insufficient space will impede the flow and scope of a lesson, and crowding will render the whole lesson potentially less safe.

2. The greater the number of pupils, the less individual attention the

instructor can give to each. This is, of course, true for flatwork as well, but, once riders are past the beginner stage, the instructor taking a lesson on the flat has greater scope for working pupils as a ride than is the case with a jumping lesson. There is an obvious connection between the amount of individual attention given and the value a pupil can derive from a lesson.

3. In a class jumping lesson, it is inevitable that pupils will sometimes have to wait their turn. The greater the number of pupils, the longer the waiting time, and the greater the likelihood of both pupils and horses 'switching off'. Admittedly, an astute instructor will seek to convince pupils of the relevance of *everything* that happens in a lesson, and to persuade them to watch and listen while others are in action. It is, however, unlikely that all pupils will prove to be paragons of keenness, and a bored, inattentive novice approaching a jump on a bored, inactive horse is a scenario which leaves much to be desired.

Regarding numbers, I know a very experienced instructor who – although a school proprietor – prefers no more than four pupils in a jumping lesson. My own opinion is that, in a standard (40 x 20 metres) arena, six is the maximum if acceptable levels of value and safety are to be maintained and – for the reasons above – this number should not be greatly surpassed in a larger arena.

CHAPTER 4

PRELIMINARY EXPLANATIONS

SINCE WE have established the important correlation between theory and practice, it will be apparent that thoughtless, uninformed practice is of little value. There is however, a tendency in British riding to rush ahead with the practical side whilst paying scant attention to the underlying principles. The result of this is that many people ride for years with little real understanding of what they are trying to achieve, and thus achieve little. This is obviously undesirable in any branch of equitation, but especially so with jumping, because of the extra element of risk involved.

Those pupils and teachers who can see the drawbacks of proceeding in this way often cite examples to indicate that the blame lies in the 'other camp'. Frustrated pupils will point to commercial stables (or even private instructors) whose attitude seems to be that none of their clients will ever be any good, and that it is therefore a waste of time trying to explain anything in detail. Teachers will claim that many pupils are impatient to 'get on with it', and seem to think that the mere fact of *doing* something (however ignorantly and incorrectly) constitutes the whole learning process.

It is undeniable that, in some cases, both parties claims are substantially true and, where instructors are at fault, it is obvious that they must make radical changes to their attitude. However, it is also important that basically conscientious instructors do not allow themselves to be railroaded into a superficial approach by impatient pupils, nor should they be tempted to devalue their teaching because of disillusionment born of generalisation. Instead, it is the instructor who must take the initiative and responsibility for establishing a programme of sound explanation and logical, measured progression. It is only by so doing that he will encourage and retain the genuinely keen pupils, and it is the achievements of such people which offer the best incentive for others to ride with greater thought, application and ambition.

The instructor will be assisted in his endeavours if he retains a clear idea of the goals he is trying to help his pupils achieve. Since we are discussing pupils who are learning the basics of jumping, the main goal must be to teach them to *ride* over jumps, as distinct from being vaguely 'able to jump' given optimum circumstances. To enlarge upon this, the aim should be to produce pupils who can ride a variety of broadly suitable horses in club/local level showjumping and cross-country events in safety and with reasonable success. Such ability will be sufficient to enable those who ride mainly for recreation to derive considerable pleasure from their jumping, and will constitute a sound basis for those whose ambitions and circumstances are such that they are keen and able to progress further.

If it is important for the instructor to have such aims clear in his own mind, it is also important that he relays them to his pupils. The reasons for this are:

1. The pupils will be helped just as much as the instructor by having specific goals and, if common goals are agreed upon, this may enhance rapport between pupil and teacher.

2. As we have seen, the observations of some novice riders may lead them to believe that jumping is a very formidable undertaking, somehow isolated from 'ordinary riding', and (however much they would like to do so) they cannot readily imagine themselves performing to any significant degree. If such pupils can be persuaded from the start that these aims are realistic, they may approach jumping with a more positive attitude than would otherwise be the case.

3. In any learning process, it is of great value if the basic principles are explained, and exercises performed, in a specific context, rather than in a 'vacuum'.

The significance of this third point must not be under-estimated. For good reasons, the environment in which riders should start jumping is somewhat benign and artificial in comparison to the showjumping arena/cross-country course/hunting field. Thus it is essential to a true learning process that gradual progress is made from a diet of basics and 'norms' in such an environment, in order for the pupil to cope with the practicalities of jumping under circumstances in which more and more variables come into play. An initial explanation of this progression will assist pupils by giving greater relevance to various exercises and instructions. To give a simple example, a pupil told to jump a single fence in a lesson may do so, but then allow the horse to stop/change gait/duck back to the rest of the ride. If he is told to maintain control of gait and direction after jumping, this constitutes correct instruction, but it will be of greater value if the instruction is put in context: 'If you were jumping a course, there might be another fence straight ahead/you might have to turn away from the collecting ring', etc.

If the teacher is to place emphasis on progression and variable circumstances, it follows that he must be precise in his instructions. He will have to make clear, as appropriate, which instructions can be considered definitive, and which pertain to a particular circumstance ('with this type of horse/this type of fence', etc.). Although this issue assumes increasingly greater relevance as riders progress, the principle should be borne in mind from the start to avoid any risk of confusing pupils with apparently contradictory advice, or leading them to believe that some action which is appropriate to one circumstance is necessarily ideal in all. (To give an analogy, it is essential that a learner driver is taught how to do an emergency stop, but it is also essential that he is not led to believe that this is the ideal way to stop at all times.)

Once pupils are aware of what they are aiming for, the next step should be to explain the broad principles of jumping. For reasons already discussed this explanation should be thorough, and ideally given while pupils are dismounted and not subject to those minor distractions which usually arise whilst preparing for a lesson.

Points to cover in general terms are:

1. All (sound, healthy) horses have a natural capacity for jumping. While actual ability will vary from horse to horse, all are capable of jumping at least moderate-sized obstacles. The natural ability of any horse will be enhanced by correct training and riding, and impaired by incorrect training and riding.

2. Those horses which are to be ridden by the pupils have been correctly trained, and are familiar with the obstacles to be jumped and the exercises to be performed. (We have already dealt with the necessity for this to be true!)

3. Riding over jumps is not an activity divorced from other branches of equitation, but it does have the obvious difference that (with the exception of some High School 'airs') it is the only branch in which the horse leaves the ground for a significant time.

The horses used should be familiar with the obstacles to be jumped. (This rider should be encouraged to keep equal weight in both stirrups.)

4. When 'jumping', most of the riding actually takes place on the flat (between jumps). During such time, it is appropriate for the rider to employ the same posture and techniques that he would normally use for such 'flatwork', in order to remain in balance and harmony with the horse, and to exercise optimum control.

5. During the act of jumping, however, a horse exhibits changes in momentum, outline and centre of gravity which differ from those exhibited during normal movement on the flat. As he approaches an obstacle, he is likely to lower his head and neck in a 'sizing up' manoeuvre. At take-off, he first pushes his forehand up with his forelegs, and then propels himself forward and up by the thrust of his hind limbs. In mid-jump, his topline should reflect the arc of his flight, with head and neck stretched forwards. At this stage, all four legs should be folded up close to his body. As he prepares to land, his forelegs, which touch down first, will unfold, and his head and neck will move somewhat up and back relative to his body, to assist his balance at the moment of landing. Once the forelegs have touched down (one just in advance of the other), the hind legs should land as much 'underneath' the horse as possible, to instigate the moving-off stride.

6. If the rider is to remain in balance, harmony and control while these changes are taking place, he must have the capacity to adapt his own posture in synchronisation with them. This *capacity* can be achieved by simple modification. The *ability* to make the appropriate adaptations comes firstly from understanding the mechanical principles involved, and secondly through practice.

While it should be emphasized that the crux of jumping lessons concerns expanding upon these points, it is important that questions relating to any of the above are actively encouraged during the instructor's explanation. This is not just a matter of ensuring that pupils understand what is being said, but also of taking the opportunity to dispel any misconceptions they have, which may become apparent through the questions. To this end, it is crucial that reasoned, logical answers are given to all questions; the instructor must not gloss over anything, nor should he give the impression that any question is foolish, however wild a misconception may lie at its root. This latter attitude will only serve to offend and embarrass the individual concerned into future silence, and discourage questions from other sources; a state of affairs conducive to neither the pupil/teacher relationship nor to the learning process itself.

CHAPTER 5

PREPARATION FOR JUMPING

AT THE START of *any* riding session, it is essential that a few minutes are spent working-in. The fundamental reason for this is to render the horse supple and responsive, but it also provides the rider with an opportunity to establish his posture, adjust his tack and collect his thoughts. At a commercial teaching establishment there is the additional consideration that working-in may allow pupils a brief period of familiarisation with horses they have perhaps never ridden before. This factor assumes greater importance when riding-in prior to jumping, and more still when pupils are about to jump for the first time. It is, in fact, a distinct advantage for pupils to have their first experiences of jumping on horses they have previously ridden in lessons on the flat, since this will reduce the number of 'new' sensations, but this, of course, is not always possible.

It is, therefore, most important that pupils are prepared for jumping by a proper and suitable period of work on the flat.

During this period the instructor should apply himself fully; it is not enough to tell novice riders 'just ride the horses round a bit and warm them up'. On the contrary, the instructor should emphasize the basic principles of equitation in the context of jumping. There are several key points on which to expand.

Active Forward Movement

Pupils *should* already understand, from their lessons on the flat, that active forward movement provides the essential basis for all correct equestrian work. This does not necessarily mean, however, that they will attempt to establish it of their own volition; indeed, it is not uncommon for inactivity to be misinterpreted as 'control' or 'collection', or just to be accepted if a rider is getting what he considers sufficient response from the horse.

In such cases, the instructor should explain that, when jumping, a horse must use himself gymnastically to propel his own and his rider's weight off the ground. This action will be made much more difficult – and less smooth – if the horse is not first moving actively forwards. The point can be expanded by explaining that an inactive horse will carry a greater proportion of his weight on his forehand, thus making it more difficult to elevate when initiating the jump, and he will also have his hind legs 'trailing', making them less effective as the agent of propulsion.

Furthermore, the presence or absence of impulsion (the horse's desire to go forward) will not only affect the ease with which active forward movement is established, but also the horse's mental attitude towards jumping (if he wants to go forward, he is more likely to jump any obstacle in his path; if he does not want to go forward, he is less likely to do so).

As ever, it is important that pupils understand that the concepts of 'activity' and 'impulsion' have to do with energy under control, and not with sheer speed. Indeed, it should be made clear that, while *energy* is essential for good jumping, *speed* (in most circumstances) is not a prime factor, and bustling a horse into a fence – or allowing him to run at it out of control – are measures which usually prove counter-productive.

Rein Contact

As is the case with the principle of active forward movement, pupils should already be aware of the need to establish and maintain a light rein contact; indeed, a correct contact (achieved by riding the horse forward onto the bit) is integral to the idea of achieving energy under control. Once again, however, there is no guarantee that pupils will automatically establish such contact; theirs may be negligible, intermittent, or otherwise inappropriate.

The instructor should explain that, to jump successfully, it is necessary both to approach an obstacle with the horse under proper control, and to maintain a light contact while he undergoes those changes of outline which occur during the jumping process. It should also be pointed out that, if a rider is unable to maintain an appropriate contact on the flat, he is most unlikely to do so whilst jumping. The instructor should, in fact, be mindful that uncorrected errors are likely to be *magnified* by jumping. He should also be aware that more serious errors are usually symptomatic of other problems which may interfere with a pupil's ability to ride over jumps – or even indicate his unreadiness to do so. In view of this, it is worth considering causes of incorrect rein contact, and their relevance in these contexts.

Lack / Loss of Contact

Apart from the reins just being too long, this may indicate:

1. Pupil misconception about not 'interfering' with the horse, which may be linked to other conceptual errors and perhaps to passive, ineffective riding.

2. Inactivity: the horse not being ridden sufficiently forward onto the bit.

3. Artificial or fixed hand positions. The most serious manifestation of this is when a rider 'plants' his hands on the withers as a result of adopting a posture whereby he is tipped forward onto his crutch, with the upper body curled forwards. Such a posture is precarious and ineffective on the flat, let alone over jumps, and *must* be corrected before the rider starts jumping.

Intermittent Contact

Indicates either:

1. Postural error, for instance upper body 'rocking' or 'bouncing' in canter, or incorrect rising trot.

2. Uneven rhythm in the horse; periodic inactivity (which may, of course, be caused/aggravated by rider's postural error).

Over-strong Contact

It is quite rare for novice riders (especially those who have had regular lessons) to take a strong contact without discernible reason.

Possible reasons for doing so are:

1. Nervousness. This must be resolved before the rider starts jumping.

2. The horse being too keen and strong for the rider to control properly. This indicates that the rider is not capable of jumping on that horse, who must therefore be replaced.

3. Serious postural errors, e.g. leaning back and hanging on to the reins. This is a definite indication that the rider needs further instruction on the flat before jumping can be considered.

Accuracy

Accuracy in riding basic figures is necessary if pupils are to approach fences along the desired line, and therefore attention should be paid to ensuring that they ride accurate circles and turns on the flat.

In particular, the errors of allowing the horse to cut corners, and of trying to prevent his doing so by pulling on the outside rein should be corrected, since the repercussions are likely to be magnified if a horse gets a little keen when jumping.

The instructor should explain that, since a jump will never be better than the approach to it, crookedness and loss of balance are to be avoided.

Because 'getting it right' with regard to the basics is crucial to success, the instructor must be prepared to return to, and expand upon, the above points as necessary throughout the teaching process. It is important that both he and the pupils keep them at the forefront of their minds, and do not make the mistake of ignoring them when pursuing other issues.

CHAPTER 6

POSTURAL ADAPTATIONS FOR JUMPING

ONCE RIDERS have worked-in to the mutual benefit of themselves and their horses, the instructor can address the issue of postural adaptations for jumping. Since it is in this area that most of the misconceptions affecting jumping tuition lie, it may be useful to re-examine the reasons that lie behind postural adaptation.

We have already seen that, when jumping, the overall aim is for the rider to remain in balance, harmony and control while the horse undergoes changes of momentum, outline and centre of gravity. The key issues relevant to this aim are:

1. To remain in balance and harmony, thus making the horse's task as easy as possible, and the jump smoother for himself, it is necessary for the rider to keep the burden of his weight as close to the horse's centre of gravity as is practical.

2. In order to retain control without interfering with the horse, the rider must be able to move his hands and arms in such a manner as to maintain a light rein contact throughout the jump. (It will be evident that such non-interfering contact will only be possible if the rider is, and feels, secure.)

To expand upon these issues, it should first be appreciated that the horse's centre of gravity is not a fixed point; indeed, its precise location changes almost continually when the horse is moving. At halt, because of the horse's conformation in general, and his long neck and head in particular, its approximate location will be vertically beneath the horse's spine, level with a point a few centimetres in front of the (normally seated) rider's knee. When the horse is in motion, the location of his centre of gravity will be

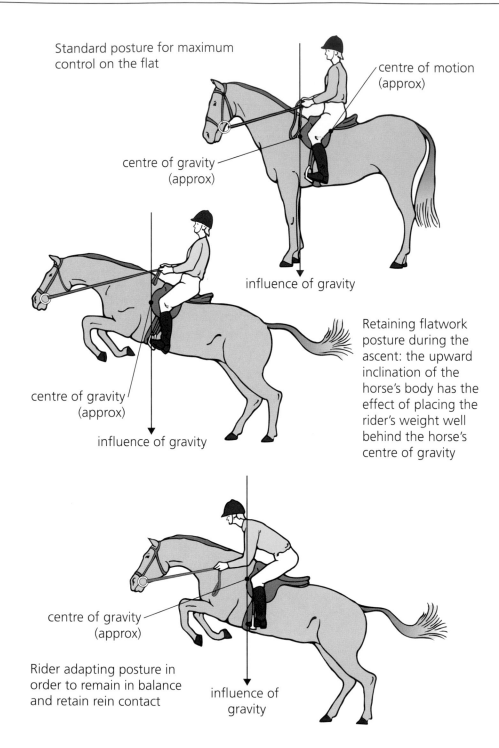

Standard posture for maximum control on the flat

centre of motion (approx)

centre of gravity (approx)

influence of gravity

Retaining flatwork posture during the ascent: the upward inclination of the horse's body has the effect of placing the rider's weight well behind the horse's centre of gravity

centre of gravity (approx)

influence of gravity

centre of gravity (approx)

Rider adapting posture in order to remain in balance and retain rein contact

influence of gravity

The need for postural adaptation when jumping

influenced by gravity itself, the effects of acceleration and deceleration, and changes in the horse's outline and weight distribution.

During the earlier (upward) stages of a jump, the acceleration generated by the thrust of take-off, and the effect of the horse stretching his head and neck forward will combine to cause the centre of gravity to move forward somewhat. Furthermore, the geometry of the jump itself will have the effect of altering the juxtaposition of the rider's weight and the horse's centre of gravity if not compensated for. This effect works thus: during the act of jumping, the horse's flight path forms an arc, with the line of his body describing, broadly speaking, a series of tangents to that arc. Therefore throughout the ascent the horse's body will be angled upward, although the actual angle will be constantly changing. Since the influence of gravity is vertically downward, if the rider were to remain in a 'normal' posture (upper body at an angle of approximately 90 degrees to the horse's topline), *any* upward inclination of the horse's body would have the effect of placing his weight further behind the horse's centre of gravity than it would be if the horse were on level ground. This effect would occur even if the horse's centre of gravity remained unaltered by the act of jumping.

If, then, the rider wishes to keep the burden of his weight as close to the horse's centre of gravity as is practical, he must compensate for these influences by folding his upper body forward *to a degree commensurate with the horse's movement.* Such action will also serve the purpose of allowing the rider to maintain a light rein contact while the horse stretches his neck and head forward during the ascent. If the rider did not fold his upper body – and thus move his shoulders – forward, his attempts to maintain the contact would be limited to movement of his hands and arms alone. While this would work passably well over very small jumps, over slightly larger ones it would cause an undesirable straightening/stiffening of the arms, with consequential loss of the valuable role played by the elbow joints in maintaining contact. In cases where the horse had to make a major effort, it would prove impossible for the rider to maintain a light contact by this means; indeed, the only way he could avoid serious interference with the horse's mouth would be to slip the reins as a matter of course.

During the descending stages of a jump, the influences described above will be reversed; the horse's centre of gravity will tend to move backward, largely as a result of his head and neck being brought up and back as a rebalancing manoeuvre, and the downward inclination of the horse's body will have the effect of placing the rider's weight nearer to the centre of gravity (or even in front of it, depending upon the rider's actual upper body

Note variations in angles A, B, C, D. For the purpose of illustration the horse's centre of gravity (•) is shown in a constant position. In practice, variations would *accentuate* the effects shown.

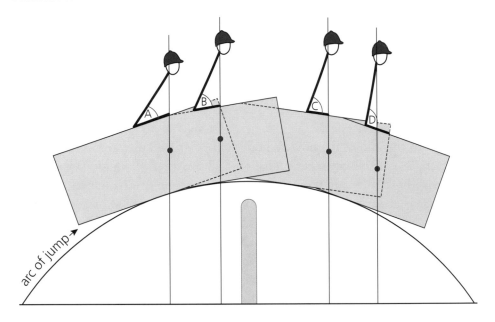

The changes in a rider's upper body posture during a jump

posture and the angles of descent). If the rider is to continue adherence to the principles of balance, harmony and control during this phase, it follows that he will have to unfold his upper body, again *to a degree commensurate with the horse's movement*.

Thus it will be apparent that the whole purpose of postural adaptation is to permit the rider to maintain dynamic balance and dynamic rein contact with the horse, and this brings us to the question of misconceptions. The two widely-held and related ones which lie at the root of much faulty jumping instruction are:

1. That there is such a thing as *the* 'jumping position'; a pre-determined posture suited to all circumstances.

2. That automatically adopting this posture during the approach to a jump is desirable/necessary.

The proposition that there is such a thing as *the* jumping position can be refuted by examining the flawed logic inherent in the idea itself. Use of the definite article 'the' implies that no alternative exists: *the* sum of two and two is inevitably four. If, then, there were such a thing as *the* jumping position, it would be possible to define it precisely; for instance, there would be a specific angle at which the rider should incline his upper body, specific angles at the elbows, etc. Since it would seem that no attempt has ever been made to define 'the jumping position' in such terms, the proposition becomes untenable.

More importantly, practical analysis of what takes place during jumping confirms that no single set posture can possibly allow a rider to remain in harmony with his horse throughout the duration of any particular jump (or even just throughout the ascent). As we have seen, the flight path of the horse, the changing inclinations of his body and his changes of outline require a *dynamic* response from the rider.

Furthermore, even if it *were* possible for a rider to adopt a set posture which allowed him to remain in harmony throughout the duration of a given jump, such a posture would not, by definition, be equally suited to a jump with a different arc. If we consider some of the variables encountered in jumping (horse's size, conformation, temperament, training, rider's ability, speed and gait of approach, ground conditions, siting of obstacle, type of obstacle, etc.) it will be apparent that the permutations which can affect a horse's jumping arc are so numerous that the idea of a 'universal' set posture becomes meaningless.

It is, of course, possible that some instructors who refer constantly to 'the jumping position' do not really believe in its existence as such, but are using a specific phrase to refer to jumping posture in general. Their reasoning may be that they are trying to 'keep things simple' for their pupils. However, while simple *truths* are of great value in teaching, over-simplification (truncating an idea to a degree where the truth becomes distorted or mislaid) is just confusing, misleading and (in our context) potentially dangerous. The point has already been made that teachers should avoid using loose terminology, and such terminology is at its most deceitful when it is disguised as precise.

Having established that there is no set 'jumping position', it will be self-evident that there is no purpose in trying to adopt such a position on the approach. Moreover, reference to the geometry of a jump will show that the philosophy behind any such attempt is flawed at its very root. This is because the rider's juxtaposition to the horse's centre of gravity is not only influenced by the rider's posture (angle of his upper body to the horse's back), but also by the inclination of the horse's body to the ground. If, for

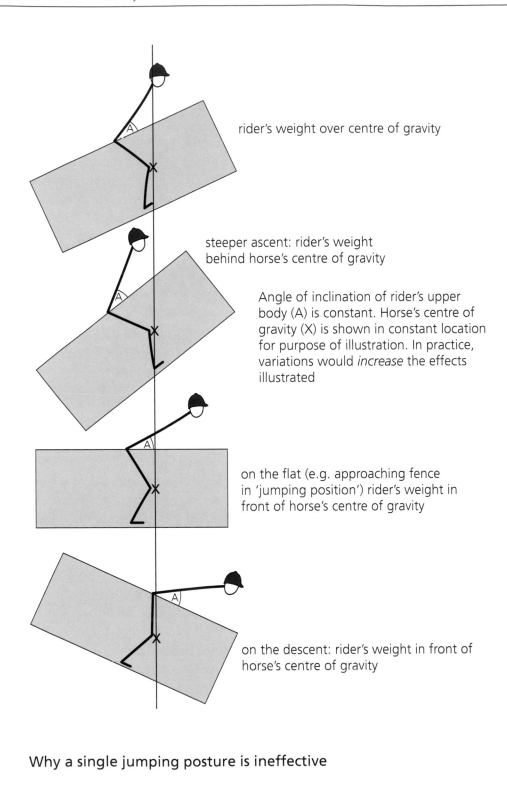

rider's weight over centre of gravity

steeper ascent: rider's weight behind horse's centre of gravity

Angle of inclination of rider's upper body (A) is constant. Horse's centre of gravity (X) is shown in constant location for purpose of illustration. In practice, variations would *increase* the effects illustrated

on the flat (e.g. approaching fence in 'jumping position') rider's weight in front of horse's centre of gravity

on the descent: rider's weight in front of horse's centre of gravity

Why a single jumping posture is ineffective

example, a rider adopted a posture which he guessed would place his weight vertically above the horse's centre of gravity when the horse was half-way through the ascent, this same posture would, on level ground, result in his weight being in front of the horse's centre of gravity; an arrangement highly precarious for the rider and of no assistance to the horse.

Once again, those who talk of approaching fences in 'the jumping position' may maintain that what they really intend is for the rider to approach in a 'forward' posture; that is, a posture of the type usually adopted when riding across country at speed. Reasons given for this proposal are that it assists the rider to fold forward on take-off, and that it will give the rider confidence. In order to establish why it is *not* a good principle to adopt such a posture automatically on the approach to a jump, we should consider the purposes and limitations of a forward posture.

We have already seen that, when seated in an upright posture, the rider's body is positioned somewhat *behind* the horse's centre of gravity, even when the horse is halted. However, in such a posture, the base of the rider's spine will be pretty much vertically above the horse's *centre of motion* (the mid-point along the horse's spine between his hind and fore limbs). This positioning allows the rider to maximize control, by enabling him to use seat and back to optimum effect, and it is therefore the best posture for occasions when maximum control is the rider's primary concern.

In other circumstances, however, different criteria apply. When a rider's main objective is to travel at speed with as little effort from the horse as possible, it follows that he should assist by making the horse's task as easy as he can. Therefore, once the required gait and speed are established, the rider should fold his upper body forward so as to place his weight closer to the horse's centre of gravity. The consequent raising of the rider's backside, so that it is poised just above the saddle, will add to the mutual comfort of horse and rider, and encourage the horse to stretch the muscles of his back and move with increased freedom.

Once a horse is settled so that he is 'cruising' – neither fighting for his head nor requiring to be kept up to his task – the rider need make little physical contribution to the partnership, beyond remaining in balance in a 'forward' posture. If, however, it becomes necessary to make significant alterations to the horse's movement – either to exercise restraint or to drive him along – the rider will need to alter his posture. If he requires to restrain the horse, he will have to reposition his weight over the horse's centre of motion in order to use his seat and/or back to full effect. If he needs to drive the horse forwards with his legs, he will first have to free his thighs from their role of supporting the folded upper body, in order that he can use his lower legs to full effect.

The truth of these points should be apparent from the instructor's own experience, but can otherwise be confirmed by observation of proficient practitioners of showjumping, horse trials, race-riding etc. The conclusion to be drawn is that a rider cannot entirely 'have it both ways'. Although he can certainly adopt postures which give some compromise between speed and control, he cannot adopt one posture which maximises both.

Therefore, while the similarities between a forward posture on the flat and postures adopted during the early stages of a jump may make the notion of approaching in a forward posture seem attractive, doing so inevitably entails forfeiting some degree of control. This is a situation unlikely to inspire rider confidence, and, as far as assisting a rider to fold foward on take-off is concerned, this depends on how and when the horse takes off, and indeed, whether he does so at all.

Although a rider who retains a forward posture throughout the approach *may* jump successfully, his doing so is largely dependent upon *all* the following criteria being met:

1. His posture on the approach must be properly in keeping with the horse's movement; that is to say he must be secure and in balance.

2. The horse must be generating genuine impulsion and thus moving actively, smoothly and rhythmically.

3. The horse must be an honest, experienced jumper, confident of tackling the type of obstacle in question.

4. The obstacle must be straightforward, both in type and siting.

5. Ground conditions must be reasonably good.

6. There must be nothing in the vicinity of the obstacle which may alarm/distract/impede the horse.

The absence of any one of these criteria will significantly increase the risk of a run-out, refusal or fall if the rider is committed to approaching in a forward posture, and instructors should be fully aware of this. Even when teaching novice pupils in a 'benign' environment (when he can exercise substantial control over the last four factors), it is pretty well impossible for an instructor to *guarantee* the presence of the first two, simply because he is dealing with pupils who are novices. In fact, extensive observation suggests

Rider 'in the middle of the horse': seat close to the saddle and lower leg in a secure position.

Below: Nobody wants a refusal but if it happens, it is preferable for the rider to stay on top of the horse. Had this rider adopted an exaggerated forward posture on the approach, she and the horse would now be on opposite sides of the fence.

that, where instructors insist upon approaches in a forward posture, the usual result is not enhanced confidence but insecurity, loss of control, confusion and disillusionment.

In the broader context of preparing pupils to jump a variety of horses in varying circumstances, to imply that a forward posture approach is the only correct method is nothing short of irresponsible.

Now that we have dealt with those avenues down which pupils should *not* be led, it is time to address the question of what they *should* be told about postural adaptation.

The instructor should reiterate the key issues of jumping already outlined, and explain that they require of the rider the facility to fold his upper body forward during the ascent, and revert smoothly and progressively to a normal posture during the descent. It should be made clear that this folding must originate from the hips, with the back kept straight, and it must be emphasized that there need not and should not be any loss of balance or security during the process.

It is at this juncture that the concept of the rider's 'platform of balance' should be introduced, together with the exercise to demonstrate the need to widen it for jumping. The instructor should explain that, in a 'normal' posture, the rider's platform of balance (represented by his seat) is not very wide. As long as the rider's posture is upright, it is quite wide enough but, once the upper body is inclined significantly in front of the vertical, the platform of balance is too narrow to maintain equilibrium. It will, instead, start to act as a pivot, with the rider's legs swinging backwards counter to the forward tilt of the upper body. With their horses suitably positioned at halt, this can be tested and proven by the pupils. They should quit their stirrups and attempt to fold their upper bodies forward as far as possible without losing balance, supporting themselves with hands on the horses' withers, or gripping unduly with their lower legs. They will discover that the degree to which they can do so is very limited.

Pupils should then be directed to draw their knees up considerably, in imitation of a jockey, and to fold forward once more. With their thighs much nearer the horizontal, the platform of balance will be substantially widened, and they will find that they can fold well forward without losing balance.

This exercise can be repeated, if necessary, with feet in stirrups and leathers being adjusted. It is important to emphasize the point that a rider will inevitably be better able to maintain balance when jumping if his leathers are shortened above his normal flatwork length. It will become

This rider has fairly short stirrup leathers, which give her a good platform of balance. Some people might criticise her 'elbows out' posture, but the fact that she has a nice, light rein contact is of far more importance.

apparent from the exercise that the shorter a rider's leathers, the wider his platform of balance will be. It is therefore necessary to explain that riding with very short leathers produces a new set of problems: it becomes difficult for the rider to sit in the saddle between fences, thus impairing his use of seat and leg aids, and it also provokes a tendency for the rider to straighten his legs when jumping, thereby pushing his body up and away from the saddle.

What is required, therefore, is a length of leather which is short enough to produce an adequate platform of balance, but not so short as to engender these difficulties. Since the physique of horse and rider and shape of saddle will influence the optimum length — and since some pupils may be riding relatively 'long' or 'short' on the flat — it is not wise for the instructor to be too dictatorial in this matter. As a starting point, he might ask all pupils to shorten their leathers by three holes, but he should then assess each individual, perhaps reiterating the folding exercise, and recommend further adjustment as appropriate.

While it is quite rare for a novice rider to over-shorten his leathers voluntarily, it is by no means uncommon to encounter resistance to shortening them sufficiently. A rider who has just succeeded in establishing an appropriate and comfortable length of leather on the flat may find that shortened leathers initially feel odd, and create a *sense* of insecurity. (In this respect, pupils who have experience of cantering outdoors, with slightly shortened leathers and modified posture, have a distinct advantage.) Resolving this issue before jumping commences is a matter of considerable importance. Allowing a pupil to retain his flat length leathers for jumping would obviously be counter-productive, but it is also unhelpful for a rider to start jumping in a negative frame of mind.

The simple solution is for pupils to spend some time riding on the flat with shortened leathers. This will not only familiarize them with the new sensation but also provide some groundwork for the riding they will have to do between jumps. Emphasis on riding simple figures and transitions accurately can help dispel any negative thoughts because of the need to concentrate upon the job in hand.

Once pupils have achieved a degree of familiarity with their shortened leathers, and while horses are moving actively forward, there is value in pupils practising folding forward from the hips. However, they should do so for *brief periods only* (three or four strides at a time), and preferably on an individual basis. For reasons already discussed, there is no useful purpose to prolonged periods practising posed 'jumping positions' and, if horses are less than ideal, such practice will serve only to provoke difficulties for the riders.

CHAPTER 7

POLE WORK AND FIRST JUMPS

IT IS NORMAL practice to introduce pupils to jumping via work over ground poles. The benefits of such work are:

1. The horse's tendency to move his head and neck forwards when traversing poles focuses attention upon the need for the rider's hands to follow such movement.

2. Riding over a series of poles focuses attention upon the need for an active and accurate approach. (The emphasis upon accuracy can be increased by the use of a matching set of striped poles.)

3. Appropriately spaced poles increase awareness of rhythm and stride length. At a later stage, they can assist pupils to meet fences on a good stride.

Poles

The poles used should be heavy and substantial — approximately 10 cm (4 in) in diameter — so that they command respect from the horses, and are not readily disturbed. For work at walk, they should be laid flat on the ground but, if certain poles are reserved for trot work, these can be stabilised further by various methods (for example, fixing wooden blocks at right angles to each end). However, such modification must not result in the *overall* height of the poles exceeding 15 cm (6 in), since this would interfere with the horses' gaits and rhythm.

If cavalletti are used for trot work, they should be set on their lowest positions: if used in an arena with a wood-based (or similarly coloured) surface, they are best painted white.

Location of Poles

When taking class lessons, it is unwise to have pupils perform exercises over poles as a ride because, if they do not keep evenly spaced, horses may become distracted, or may not be able to see the poles, and the instructor may have insufficient time to replace any dislodged poles. However, it is also preferable, whenever possible, to avoid having pupils perform one at a time while the rest of the ride is halted, since this interferes with continuity and induces loss of concentration in both horses and riders.

Such drawbacks can be avoided by locating poles so that individuals can be nominated from a moving ride, perform the exercise, and return to the ride. In the early stages, the simplest location is on the inside track, with the outer ends of the poles two metres or so from the arena perimeter. There is a school of thought which suggests that poles are best placed on the outside track, so that the arena wall acts as a continuous wing. However, although this is a good idea in theory, the majority of arenas have a significant track worn close to the walls, into which horses tend to 'fall' unless ridden with considerable accuracy and determination. Therefore, if poles are placed across this track, it may prove difficult for riders to aim for the centre of the poles as they should.

Although it allows for four different approaches, placing poles across the centre line (AC) is not a good idea, since any loss of impulsion or inaccuracy on the turn will affect the quality of the approach. Placing poles on a long diagonal (KM or HF) is useful for emphasizing the need for rhythm and accuracy, but is more suited for teaching an individual pupil, since the change of rein can create problems in returning to a class ride.

Spacing Between Poles

Since pole work should emphasize impulsion, rhythm, balance and stride length, it follows that these qualities should not be impaired by inappropriate spacing of the poles themselves. For horses of average stride length, poles should be placed approximately 0.8 metres apart for exercises at walk, and approximately 1.3 metres apart for trot. Pupils must not, therefore, be required to walk over poles set for trotting, or vice versa.

With class lessons, it is probable that there will be some variation in stride lengths between the various horses employed. If these are relatively slight, the instructor can use one set of poles, spaced to favour the longer-striding animals. Where there is a marked disparity, however, it will be necessary to provide two sets of poles, each spaced as appropriate. If this is done in a standard width arena, it is best to place the two sets on opposite inside

It is important that trotting poles are placed to suit the individual horse.

tracks, since placing them side by side will make the approach turn to the inner set rather tight.

Walking Over Poles

Walking over a few single poles introduces pupils to the need for an active gait in order for the horse to negotiate them cleanly, and highlights the need for the rider's hands to respond to movement of the horse's head. As soon as pupils are proceeding satisfactorily, they can progress to a series of poles, which will emphasize these points, together with the need for a straight approach, and provide a link into trotting over a series of poles.

Trotting Over Poles

In the context of teaching riders to jump, most pole work will be performed in rising trot, and pupils should proceed to this once the work at walk is satisfactory. After trotting a couple of times over a single pole for familiarisation, they can be introduced to a series of poles.

The ideal number to begin with is four; negotiated by two full strides of trot, thus being instructive but not over-demanding. The use of just two

Active trot through poles. The horse's footfalls, central between the poles, show that they have been spaced correctly for this individual.

poles is to be avoided, since horses may occasionally attempt to jump both. The instructor must emphasize the need for impulsion and rhythm, and ensure that these qualities are present *before* each pupil approaches the poles. Over the poles themselves, pupils need be asked to do no more than maintain the quality of the trot. Any postural errors should, however, be corrected. It is especially important to cure any tendency to rise too high at this juncture, since this error causes loss of balance, impairing the rider's ability to fold forward correctly once the jumping stage is reached. It may also cause an uneven, intermittently harsh rein contact, which will hinder the horse and discourage rhythmic forward movement.

First Jumps

Once pupils are negotiating the trotting poles in good style, a very small jump can be introduced. This should consist of crossed poles, about 25 cm high at the centre, which should be accurately aligned with the centres of the trotting poles. The distance from the last of the trotting poles to the base of the fence should be twice the distance between the trotting poles themselves. If it has been necessary to use two sets of poles for the trotting exercises, their use should continue, each with a fence set at the appropriate distance. In such cases, the instructor should ensure that both fences are designed to be taken on the same rein. The provision of wings will help concentrate the horses' minds, and thus assist their riders.

Pupils should be told to trot over the poles exactly as before: on clearing the last pole, they should sit in the saddle and squeeze the horse's sides with their legs. As the horse takes off, they should fold the upper body forward a little, and allow their hands and arms to respond to the movement of the horse's head. Legs must remain on the girth. Timing can be assisted by pupils saying to themselves '1, 2, 3, 4, sit, fold', the sequence starting as they reach the first pole.

The need to give the leg aid should be emphasized. It should be explained that, if a rider wishes a horse to do something, he must *ask* him to do it. This applies to jumping, just as to all other movements. As with other aids, the optimum application of the jumping aids will vary, the chief influences being the characteristics of the horse and the characteristics of different obstacles. Although, at this juncture, only light aids should be necessary, they should

A placing pole to a cross-pole. The rider is standing slightly in the stirrups, and her seat is rather a long way out of the saddle.

still be given; it will set a dangerous precedent if pupils are led – even tacitly – to believe that horses will always take off automatically.

So far as the actual jump is concerned, the instructor should bear in mind that, while it provides the pupils' first experience of leaving the ground, the horses efforts will be very slight. Therefore, whilst looking for evidence that pupils are conforming to the principles of jumping, he should remember that these involve rider response appropriate to the horse's actions; unnecessary extravagances should be neither expected nor condoned.

Continuing with this line of thought, it must be recognized that, from the moment of the first jump, a rider will start to form habits, whether good or bad. The wise instructor will, therefore, seek to encourage the former and eradicate the latter from this very early juncture. There is no point in accepting as satisfactory anything short of correctness; if errors are ignored they will quickly become ingrained, and inevitably worsen as fences get bigger.

It is, of course, easier to identify and evaluate errors once they become marked, but this is not a good reason for ignoring them until then! Indeed, it is characteristic of a good teacher that he will correct incipient errors, not wait until they are full-blown before noticing them. This is not to say that

Over poles, the rider's hands need
to respond to the position of the horse's head

errors will *only* start to manifest themselves in the early stages, but simply that, while the instructor must remain constantly vigilant, he must be so from the very beginning. It is for this reason that we should take an early look at common jumping errors.

Jumping Errors

It is very easy for an instructor, in any sphere of equitation, to identify peripheral faults and say 'don't do this, stop doing that'. In many cases, however, these faults are merely symptomatic of a more fundamental error, and it is this which should be the focal point of the instructor's attention. In addition to the obvious need to correct such errors, doing so will alleviate or cure the symptomatic faults. Contrastingly, it may be physically impossible for a pupil to correct a symptomatic fault without first resolving the root cause, and attempts to do so may actually aggravate the underlying problem and/or provoke new ones. Following on from this, it may be that several symptomatic faults have the same underlying cause, and dealing with this will result in dramatic overall improvement. On the other hand, subjecting the pupil to a fusillade of unrelated, arbitrary instructions will just cause confusion and disillusionment.

The following analysis may help in establishing the causes of jumping errors, and effecting their cures.

Errors Associated with Loss of Impulsion on the Approach

Symptoms
Horse jumps clumsily, either with minimal effort, or with extra, last moment effort. Rider out of balance either in front of, or substantially behind horse's centre of gravity displaying various associated symptoms.

Root Causes and Cures
1. Under-riding. Rider not asking for sufficient activity from horse. This *may* be due to lack of understanding – although it is unlikely that this would manifest itself suddenly at this juncture. If this does seem to be the cause, the instructor can use the resultant poor jump to illustrate the need for an active approach. However, under-riding is more likely to occur because the horse is too big/clumsy/sluggish for the rider *or* because he is too keen/strong and the rider is trying to keep him quiet by doing nothing. At an early stage of training, these causes are best dealt

Rider errors at a jump

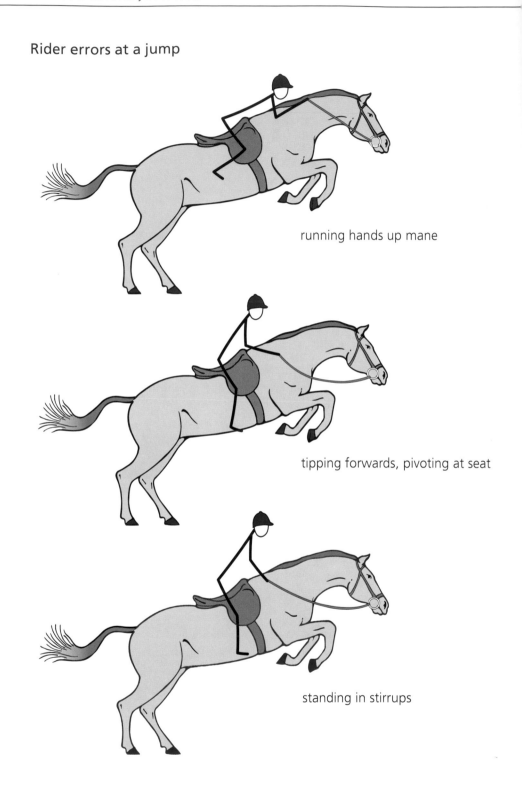

running hands up mane

tipping forwards, pivoting at seat

standing in stirrups

Rider errors at a jump

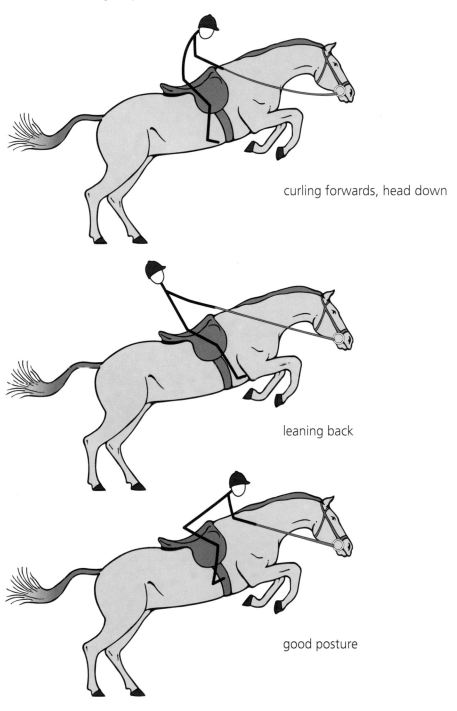

curling forwards, head down

leaning back

good posture

with by changing the horse. If this is really not possible, the instructor must do all he can to help and encourage the pupil, not pretend he is ideally mounted and expect perfection.

2. Rider ceasing to ask for active movement through preoccupation with jump. Associated with rider 'freezing' in front of jump and not giving an aid for take-off. This may occur in a perfectionist pupil who is over-concerned about thinking ahead and getting it right, or it may indicate nervousness or confusion resulting from past teaching. The cure is to convince the pupil to keep riding right up to take-off. Since a horse so ridden will inevitably jump in better style, those rider faults which were engendered by a bad jump will no longer be in evidence.

3. Rider anticipating take-off. This has links with the above, but is typified by the rider attempting to adopt a forward posture on the approach, and thus impairing his ability to keep the horse moving actively forwards. The cure is to tell the pupil to concentrate on maintaining the quality of the gait on the approach, and to 'wait' for the obstacle.

Instructional Errors to Avoid
Attending exclusively to errors of posture over jump, when they are almost inevitable consequences of the incorrect approach. (At this juncture, we are considering jumps with regulated approaches, and therefore errors associated with crooked, unbalanced and over-fast approaches will be dealt with in due course.)

Errors Associated with Rider Unbalancing Forwards Over Jump

Symptoms
The ultimate symptom is the rider falling off over the horse's shoulder; irrefutable proof that his weight was in front of the horse's centre of gravity. This may occur if various faults are exaggerated.

Root Causes and Cures

1. Running hands up horse's mane, upper body tilted far forward, legs swinging up and back behind the girth. The cause is that the rider has the reins too short on the approach, and then makes a desperate effort to avoid hardening the contact during the jump itself. This problem is often associated with the rider of a keen/strong horse being reluctant to give

him his head, and therefore should not arise during the early stages of jumping tuition. If it does, the simple solution is to change the horse, and the educational cure is to teach the pupil control by riding 'leg into hand', rather than attempting restraint with the reins alone. If the pupil is riding with reins too short for no apparent reason, he can simply be told to lengthen them.

2. Upper body tipped far forward, legs swinging back, hands planted on horse's withers. Rein contact usually lost. This is caused by the rider pivoting from his seat rather than folding from the hips, and is associated with over-long stirrup leathers creating a narrow platform of balance. The fault can be cured by adjusting the length of leathers as appropriate, and by teaching the pupil to keep his legs on the girth and to fold the upper body correctly.

3. Standing in stirrups, straightening legs, toes pointed down, backside raised far out of saddle, hands planted on withers to prevent/redress loss of balance. The root cause is misconception; the rider thinking that he can help the horse to elevate by elevating himself. The cure is to convince the rider of his misconception: reference to the laws of physics will show that his effort in pushing himself up is matched by a downward thrust which will materially *hinder* the horse. It may help the pupil to break this habit if he has a mental image of remaining 'kneeling' over the jump.

   This error may also be associated with/aggravated by attempting to retain over-long stirrups. On the other hand, if a rider with this fault has his leathers too *short* he is likely to become unbalanced backwards (see next section).

4. Upper body curled forward (i.e. spine curved), head down, hands either tucked into lap or resting on pommel/withers. The problems with curling rather than folding forwards are that the rider's seat is loosened and it is inherently harder to uncurl than to unfold on the descent. Pupils with this fault will fall off readily if the horse jumps awkwardly, especially if there is marked deceleration at the moment of landing. The main symptoms are inter-related; if the spine is curled forwards, the head will look down – if the rider looks down, it is highly likely that the spine will curl forwards. Curling forwards may be simply the result of a misconceived attempt at folding the upper body, and looking down may be sheer habit born of curiosity. Frequently, however, both faults are associated with a defensive attitude. Where this is suspected, the underlying reasons

must be investigated and resolved. From the mechanical point of view, the pupil may be assisted by having an image of pushing his stomach towards his thighs as an aid for correct folding, and by fixing his gaze on an eye-level object beyond the jump as an aid for keeping his head up. (In the latter case, the instructor may, for example, hold up a hand and ask 'how many fingers?.)

How many fingers?

Instructional Errors to Avoid
Glossing over these faults on the grounds that 'at least the pupil is not interfering with the horse's mouth' or 'he's got the general idea about going forwards over a jump'. Such thinking does the pupils no favours whatsoever, and tacit acceptance of these faults may contribute towards a future accident.

Errors Associated with Rider's Weight Remaining Significantly Behind the Horse's Centre of Gravity

Symptoms
Rider leans, or appears to lean backwards. Arms straightened, hands sometimes raised, rein contact hardened (if reins not slipped) – in severe cases to the extent that rider is literally hanging on by the reins. Legs thrust forwards.

Root Causes and Cures

1. Rider caught out by horse standing off (taking off abnormally far from the jump) unexpectedly. This is unlikely when the approach is regulated by poles unless the horse makes a sudden effort after losing impulsion. Causes of loss of impulsion on the approach have already been examined. Other aspects of the approach which may have a bearing on this problem will be considered in due course. For the moment, it should be borne in mind that, while a horse standing off should not cause these symptoms in a rider who has asked him to do so, his doing so unexpectedly almost certainly will. Therefore, providing a pupil only exhibits these symptoms under such circumstances, it is his riding of the *approach* which requires investigation.

2. Rider with tendency to stand in the stirrups over jumps has his leathers too short. The action of standing lifts him so far out of the saddle that he is literally left behind in the air. (This fault has parallels with the error of rising excessively high when trotting.) The cure is to adjust the leathers and deal with the misconception as previously discussed.

3. Trepidation. Rider frightened of the jump (or jumping in general), perhaps because of past experience. This must be investigated tactfully and resolved before pupil continues, otherwise the consequences are likely to be detrimental to both horse and rider.

Instructional Errors to Avoid
Simply telling the pupil to 'get forward'. Given in isolation, this instruction does nothing to resolve the underlying causes, and is likely to provoke further problems.

In the case of a horse who has made extra effort after an inactive approach, giving this advice next time may cause the pupil to anticipate take-off and stop riding, so that the horse arrives at the fence with even less impulsion than before, and with the rider dangerously far forward. In any circumstances, a rider who flings himself extravagantly forward on the assumption that his mount will stand off is likely to go on alone if the horse puts in an extra stride (or refuses!) instead. Furthermore, the sudden over-burdening of his forehand may well influence the horse's decision and, in any case, will almost certainly cause him to jump flat. In the case of a nervous pupil, merely telling him to 'go forward' (however much he may need to do so) is an instruction he will either ignore, or obey half-heartedly and incorrectly, with negative results.

There is also a conceptual mistake which instructors should avoid, and this is to assume that a rider whose weight remains somewhat behind the horse's gravity is *inevitably* committing an error. Under the regulated circumstances of early jumping instruction, a pupil who sits back almost certainly *is* at fault and, if he pulls the horse in the mouth, the fault is very serious indeed. At some stage, however, pupils will almost certainly encounter circumstances in which it is prudent or even necessary to keep the weight back somewhat. Examples include: jumping drop fences (especially into water), conviction that a horse is about to hit a fence hard, and riding horses which (for whatever reason) are reluctant to jump. Under such conditions, attempting to keep the weight directly above the horse's centre of gravity entails an unacceptable degree of risk, and an instructor who expects pupils to do so is simply endangering them through his own lack of understanding. (It is, of course, essential that riders learn to slip their reins properly before encountering such conditions, and we will consider this matter in due course.)

CHAPTER 8

PROGRESSION

Up to this point it is beneficial, whenever practical, for exercises to be carried out with the whole class on the move. During the ensuing stages, however, considerations of space and safety will generally necessitate individual performances, and these will be essential where a relatively large class is being taught in a standard size arena.

Preliminary Considerations

Two points arise from this:

1. Pupils not currently performing should be encouraged to observe those who are, and be positioned where they can do so readily without causing interference.

2. There must be room and opportunity for those who have been waiting their turn to get their mounts moving actively forwards before jumping. Waiting for several minutes, then riding round one corner to take a fence, is *not* a recipe for success.

As long as pupils are performing jumping exercises which utilise trotting poles, placing poles and related distances, the rationale of providing alternatives for horses of markedly different stride lengths must continue. Furthermore, the instructor must be prepared, if necessary, to adjust distances in the light of a horse's capabilities, rather than seeking to impose textbook distances where they do not suit. The purpose of using placing poles and related distances is, at this stage, to *assist* pupils by ensuring that their horses jump out of a smooth, even stride. This purpose will not be served by providing inappropriate spacings, and there is no sense in doing so and then criticizing pupils for errors induced by such spacings. While it is certainly important that, in due course, pupils are taught to identify and cope with awkward approaches and distances, they must be taught the basics first.

Progressing from the First Jump; Jumping from Canter

Once pupils are negotiating the first jump in good style, the next step is to increase the height in stages to about 40 cm. The best way to do this is to add a ground line, and place a single pole on auxilliary stands immediately behind the crossed poles. This will provide an obstacle of fairly substantial, but inviting, appearance.

If any horses offer canter on landing, their riders should be told to allow two or three strides before returning to trot. This is preferable to expecting pupils to retain trot, or regain it immediately, since such demands may cause them to hang on to their mounts during the approach, with detrimental consequences. On the other hand, it is a serious error if pupils permit their horses to fall into walk, or veer towards the rest of the ride after jumping. Such occurrences can be emphasized and corrected by placing two cones adjacent to the quarter marker after the jump, each about one metre either side of a straight line extended from the centre of the jump. Pupils can then be required to trot between these cones after jumping, any deviation from this requirement being self-evident.

Once pupils can maintain gait and direction after the jump, the next step is to approach in canter. If the first, third and fourth trotting poles (counting from the approach side) are removed, the remaining pole should provide one non-jumping canter stride between itself and the fence (though its position should be adjusted if this proves necessary).

The instructor should explain that the principles of jumping from canter are the same as for trot and that, even though everything will take place a little faster, the jump itself is likely to be smoother. The timing of aids and take-off can be assisted by pupils thinking 'squeeze and fold', starting as their horses cross the placing pole; if there is any tendency to look down, the instructor can assist by giving such commands himself. It is important that horses arrive at the fence with a good even rhythm established, and pupils must be given time, room and any assistance necessary to achieve this. However, there are two eventualities which the instructor should guard against. These are:

1. Every effort should be made to ensure that no rider is 'taken' at the jump by an over-enthusiastic horse. On the one hand, such experience can

Using the arena

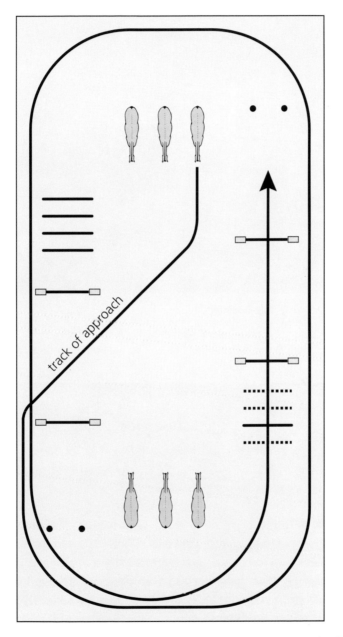

track of approach

Two sets of poles and jumps laid out to accommodate horses of differing stride lengths. Left side: approach over trotting poles. Right side: approach in canter over spacing poles. Track of approach allows time to establish active gait after period of waiting.

A placing pole to a cross-pole in canter.

Below: On this occasion, the placing pole has not really worked; the horse has taken off too far from the cross-pole. Because the fence is so low, he will doubtless clear it, but he would be struggling over a bigger obstacle.

prove alarming for a novice, and may provoke serious errors on the approach if the rider just hangs on to the horse's head. On the other hand, a more intrepid personality who jumps successfully despite being 'taken' may be misled into believing that the key to riding an approach is simply to sit there and abandon control.

If, then, the instructor feels that a horse is likely to take charge, the pupil should be told to ride one or more 15 metre circles in trot at the end of the arena before the jump, and to ask for canter only at that point between completion of the circle and approaching the placing pole which the instructor deems appropriate. Once canter *is* taken, however, the pupil must be encouraged to ride forwards positively.

2. It may be necessary to emphasize the distinction between an active canter and any tendency to bustle a horse into a long, flat outline: the latter being an early example of the common error of approaching fences too fast from too far out.

After the jump, the principle of maintaining gait and direction should be continued, with at least six more canter strides before a correct transition to trot. This is important, because pupils must think of the jump as taking place within the context of riding as a whole, and not as an isolated end in itself. The next stage, indeed, is to reinforce this idea by adding a second fence. Since the object is still to make the actual jumping process as easy as possible, this should be at a related distance from the first. Some experienced instructors believe that it is best to provide a one stride double straight away, on the grounds that the single stride gives an ungenerous horse less opportunity to run out or 'fiddle'. While the logic of this idea is undeniable, my own feeling is that moving directly from a single obstacle to a one stride double is rather demanding of the pupils, who may get caught out or flustered into error. A two stride double gives riders more time and space, and encourages them to sit down and ride the distance between the jumps. Furthermore, since one *hopes* that the horses being used are of a reasonably generous nature, any difficulties are most likely to arise from pupil error in this respect. They can therefore be used to illustrate the need to ride for the *final* element of any combination and, by extention, to be positive on the approach to any jump.

When building an initial two stride combination, there are three points to bear in mind:

1. The second element should be similar to the first, to encourage rider confidence through familiarity.

2. Pupils should be *told* the number of non-jumping strides between elements. This will not only help their first efforts, but also introduce them to the idea of assessing distances.

3. As already mentioned, the distance must be right *for the horses and circumstances*. If teaching at a riding school, it is likely that the instructor will be dealing with horses of no great scope who, at this stage, are jumping very small obstacles. Furthermore, the aim is for them to retain a reasonably rounded outline, and to jump without reaching for the fences. Therefore, rather than seeking to apply a notional distance regardless, it makes sense to refer to the spacing which has already proved correct in the current conditions; that between the placing pole and the first fence. If the second fence is positioned so that the distance between it and the first fence is one and two-thirds times the distance between the placing pole and the first fence, very little adjustment should prove necessary. (At a later stage, when bigger fences and spreads are built in combinations, distances will, of course, have to be increased as appropriate.)

The primary purpose of the combination is, at this juncture, to provide a simple introduction to the idea of jumping more than one fence at a time; it is not, specifically, to introduce pupils to the concept of gymnastic jumping. I do not feel, therefore, that too much emphasis need be placed on further combination work as yet. With regard to jumping-lanes, my opinion is that they are excellent for educating horses, and for assisting somewhat more experienced riders to hone technique. In any but a most basic form, however, they can be too intricate and demanding for use as a first phase introduction for novice riders.

The next step after jumping two fences in a straight line is to jump two fences (still with placing poles) set on opposite sides of the arena. In theory, this is most simply done by pupils jumping the first fence, then continuing in canter on the same rein to jump the second. Given the right circumstances, this is a useful enough exercise. In some arenas, however, it may not be straightforward; this applies especially to 40 x 20 metre arenas which have well-worn outside tracks and no safe way of using the arena walls as wings.

Jumping two fences on opposite sides of the arena

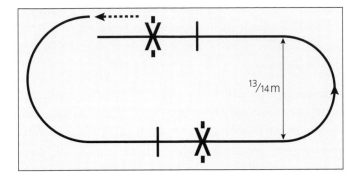

Fences with wings set on inside track. The turn in canter is rather tight for novice riders.

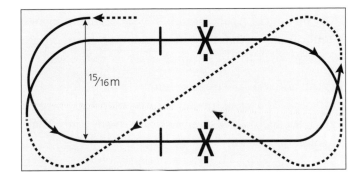

Fences with wings set on inside track, jumped from canter with changes of rein in trot. Diameter of turns into fences increased.

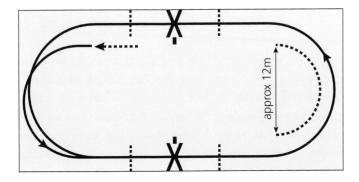

Fences using arena walls as wings. Applicable only where arena construction and surface are appropriate. Allows wide turns into fences but restricts turns on the flat.

The difficulties are:

1. If fences on both sides of the arena are built with conventional wings, and positioned so that they can be bypassed on the outside track, the turn between them will be rather tighter than desirable at this stage (approximately 13–14 metres).

2. Building fences with their wings *on* the outside track interferes with general movement around the arena, and, if the outside track is deeply worn, the resultant fence tends to be both tilted and unstable. More seriously, however, any rider whose horse finds the outside track a magnetic attraction will be confronted, not by an inviting jump, but by the wing itself.

3. If it is possible to use the arena wall/fence in place of a wing, a deeply worn outside track may still lead to approaches closer to the wall than to the centre of the fence. Apart from being incorrect in principle, this can lead to complications with fences incorporating crossed poles (the horse is likely to 'skew' over them, jumping away from the wall).

    N.B. if a post and rail perimeter fence, which does not incorporate proper jump cups, is used as a wing, jump poles must be positioned with great care; if wedged against an upright post, they make the fence effectively solid.

It will be seen, then, that in many arenas an apparently simple exercise can prove problematical. One way to circumvent such problems is to incorporate a change of rein; pupils jump the first fence from canter, change the rein across the long diagonal through trot, then canter over the second fence. Even with conventionally-winged fences built on the inside tracks, this makes more space, since the rider can *start* approaches to both jumps on the outside tracks. Although, compared to remaining on one rein, some continuity of jumping is lost, this exercise can still be extended so that each fence is jumped more than once. Furthermore, it promotes the principle of jumping within a controlled programme of flatwork, and the changes of rein will lessen the likelihood of problems associated with horses anticipating (cutting corners, rushing fences, carelessness and not listening to their riders).

Unsatisfactory fence construction

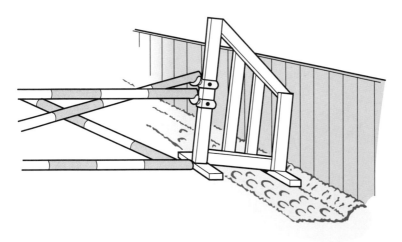

Wings placed in deep outside track: unstable and potentially dangerous

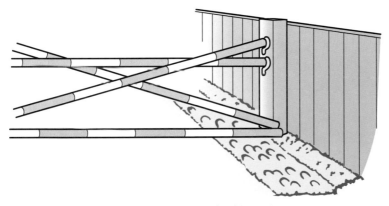

Deep outside track encouraging crooked jumping

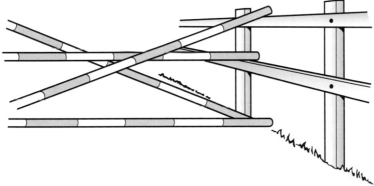

Jump poles wedged against posts making fence virtually solid

Towards Bigger Fences

Up to this point, we have been concerned with introducing pupils to the first principles of taking jumps; everything, including the fences themselves, having been made as easy as possible, so that they can concentrate fully on absorbing these principles. The next step is to focus more attention on the obstacles themselves, and familiarize pupils with relatively bigger fences. This serves two purposes: firstly, to *increase* confidence in the act of jumping and secondly, by so doing, to render pupils more receptive to criteria other than size which must be considered when evaluating and jumping obstacles. (If a rider *knows* that he can jump a fence larger than that being incorporated into a particular exercise, he is more likely to concentrate upon the whole exercise rather than just worry about the jump.)

Although, at present, we are still considering fences which are really pretty small, this may be an appropriate moment to consider the concept of over-facing. Any sensible trainer – of horses or riders – will take great care to avoid over-facing his charges; as far as his pupils are concerned, this means that he will not ask them to tackle obstacles requiring levels of confidence and technical ability which they do not yet possess. However, *developing* ability and confidence is fundamental to any teaching process, and a jumping instructor is doing pupils no favours by using the issue of over-facing as an excuse never to raise fences above knee height. (It has also to be said that, at some riding schools, pupils never get a chance to develop their confidence because the horses are so ill-schooled and unsuitable that *they* are over-faced by anything higher than cavalletti.)

What an instructor should do, therefore, is progress towards bigger fences, but with great care and deliberation. The twin essentials are:

1. That he is absolutely certain that the horses used will jump the obstacles willingly, given half a chance.

2. While he remains acutely receptive to any signs of mental or physical difficulty on the pupils' part, he is fundamentally obliged to call a halt *before* any such signs are manifest.

It is not, of course, sensible to *start* a jumping lesson by introducing pupils to fences larger than they have faced before; there should be a few warm-up exercises of the type previously performed. Furthermore, no great issue should be made of the fact that fences are about to get bigger: shouting 'right, it's puissance time – who's got a parachute?' may raise some forced smiles, but is unlikely to raise confidence levels. Instead, the introduction should be along the lines of 'now we've done a few exercises on approaching and getting away from fences, we're going to concentrate a bit more on the actual jumping'.

Similarly, the instructor should ease pupils unobtrusively into the *act* of jumping bigger fences. This can be initiated simply by continuing the exercise of taking a single fence from canter (with a placing pole), while gradually increasing the dimensions. The value of increasing spread as well as height should not be overlooked, since greater spread will produce more scopey jumps from the horses, thus giving pupils the feel of a bigger jump without making the fence look much bigger. It should be remembered that, assuming the placing pole is correctly located to begin with, increases in spread should be made by moving the back pole, and not by bringing the ground line forwards. (As size increases, it is preferable to employ placing poles which give two or three – appropriate length – strides in front of fences, so that any horse meeting a placing pole 'wrong' has more room for adjustment.)

While pupils are taking the larger fences, the instructor should stress adherence to those principles already practised, but he must also be watchful for any errors appearing or being magnified. It is important that the size of the fence is not increased every time pupils jump it, since this would over-emphasize the issue. It is also important not to go too far in a single lesson. Assuming that the equipment allows for height increases of 5 or 6 cm at a time, three increases in the first lesson – with corresponding increases in spread – should represent significant progress without being over-demanding. Such increases cannot, obviously, be maintained *ad infinitum*, and subsequent lessons must take account of pupils' progress and horses' abilities.

Once pupils are jumping pole fences slightly higher than the basic 'fillers' available, these 'fillers' can be incorporated to introduce the pupils to more solid fences. The best way to use them is to insert them in front of the back pole of an existing fence (e.g. in place of cross poles), so that they can be shown – despite their solid appearance – to be lower than the fence already jumped. Once 'fillers' have been introduced, the instructor has the wherewithal to provide a greater variety of obstacles without necessarily employing (and moving!) so many poles. He should, in the early stages, however, continue to favour fences which slope a little away from the direction of approach. He should also remember that only ground poles should be located in front of 'fillers', otherwise a false groundline will be created.

The process of building confidence over larger jumps should be continued at *occasional* intervals, subject to the constraints already mentioned. It is important that neither teacher nor pupils become obsessed with height, and a 'get over it regardless' attitude must never substitute regard for sound technique. Furthermore, for reasons already given, the fact that pupils have successfully jumped fences of a certain size does not mean to say that such fences should automatically or usually be employed in subsequent lessons. Indeed, the major part of lesson time should be concerned with aspects of jumping other than size, and we shall consider these in due course.

Slipping the Reins

While jumping straightforward fences on good ground, with a regulated approach, it is unlikely that the need to slip the reins will arise. Such conditions, however, will not necessarily be pertinent once pupils have passed the basic stage, and they will need to understand the principles of slipping the reins before they can cope safely and effectively with any of the following:

- Meeting an obstacle on a bad stride.

- Horse hitting an obstacle hard.

- Horse stumbling for any reason.

- Jumping drop fences – especially into water or mud.

Since the first of these circumstances (and conceivably the next two) may arise as soon as pupils start tackling fences without placing poles, it makes sense to introduce them to the idea of slipping the reins *before* failure to do so causes problems for themselves or their horses. The purpose of slipping the reins can be explained from the viewpoint of both horse and rider. As far as the horse is concerned, it is the means by which he can be allowed extra rein if he stands off a fence unexpectedly, lands steeply, or is otherwise in danger of losing his balance. It allows the rider to place his weight sufficiently far behind the horse's centre of gravity to counter the effects of sudden deceleration or an unduly steep landing without hardening the rein contact.

Opposite, above: A secure posture over a bigger fence. The rider is sitting 'in the middle of the horse', but allowing him the freedom to jump.

Opposite, below: This horse has jumped rather high over the wall, but has not tucked up his legs; a novicy or uncertain effort. To become effective, a rider must learn how to adapt quickly to moments of imperfection.

(It should be explained that, although this course of action is contrary to the normal principles of jumping, there may be times when it is necessary if the rider is to avoid a fall.)

The practice of slipping the reins can be defined as opening the fingers sufficiently to allow the horse to take extra rein the moment it becomes necessary for him to do so. Some sensitive pupils may have done this subconsciously if their mount has ever stumbled on the flat, but the nearest equivalent action they may have learnt in the school is that of allowing a horse to 'take' the rein contact forward and down after a period of concentrated work. Although 'giving and retaking' the reins is normally done in a more leisurely fashion than slipping them, the exercise can be used to accustom pupils to the idea and 'feel'.

It is most important that pupils are taught to slip their reins because, where it is necessary, the alternatives – hanging on to the horse's mouth or committing themselves to highly precarious postures – are very unattractive. The subject should be reiterated and expanded when pupils begin jumping across country, where terrain and ground conditions make the need for this skill most prevalent.

Dispensing with Placing Poles

The object of using placing poles in early exercises is to ensure that pupils meet their fences on a good stride, so that they have only to concern themselves with their own actions in the context of a smooth jump, and do not have to worry about adapting or responding to the effects of jumping off an indifferent stride. However, outside the boundaries of the teaching arena, obstacles do not have placing poles so, once pupils are jumping confidently and in good style, it is necessary to wean them off such assistance.

It should be noted that this order of progression is far preferable to starting pupils off with an unregulated approach and no knowledge – because of their inexperience – of how to assess or regulate their own progress. Coupling such an introduction with criticizing a pupil one moment for being 'left behind' if his horse stands off a fence, and the next moment telling him to 'wait for a jump' if the horse puts in an extra stride, is a recipe for total confusion.

This leads us to the question of *how* to dispense with placing poles without causing any confusion of this type. In the first instance, although placing poles cannot physically fade away they can, in a sense, disappear by degrees. The instructor may, for example, provide two similar fences, initially retaining the placing pole at one of them, so that it acts as a reminder for pupils. He can also, for a while, substitute cones (one where each end of the pole was) to retain a visual indication to pupils of the last stride before the jump. Such measures are, however, for short term guidance. The instructor's main task is to replace any need for placing poles with the knowledge and experience which will allow pupils to adapt to the different efforts made by their mounts in different circumstances, and, later, to influence and regulate the approach itself.

The first step along this path consists of background explanation. Pupils should be told that, now they have a sound grasp of the basic facts and sensations of jumping, it is time to start learning how to adapt to the circumstances they will encounter beyond the confines of the teaching arena. At this point, the precise role of placing poles can be expanded upon, so that pupils understand not just that they regulate the approach, but how they do so. The instructor should explain that every fence has a take-off zone; the area in front of it from which a horse should take off to maximize his chance of a successful jump. Since the arc of a jump must be related to what a horse is jumping, it follows that the take-off point must be related to the dimensions of any given fence. For most types of fence, the take-off zone is reckoned to be between 1 and 1½ times the maximum height of the fence from a point vertically beneath its maximum height. Thus, if a horse is to jump an upright fence 1 metre high, he should take off somewhere between 1 and 1½ metres from its base. It must be emphasized that a horse *may* clear a fence if he takes off either a little closer or somewhat further away than the take-off zone, but that taking off within the zone allows him to jump smoothly and with minimum effort.

The purpose of placing poles is to regulate the horse's approach so as to ensure that he takes off within the prescribed zone. If there is no such guidance, the horse/rider partnership have to make their own efforts to arrive there. Left to his own devices, a horse may follow one of two basic courses:

1. Adjust his own stride during the approach so as to take off from an appropriate point.

2. Approach on an even stride. If he happens to arrive within the take-off zone, he will jump smoothly, otherwise he will either take off abnormally far from the fence (stand off) and make an extra effort, or take off abnormally close and jump very steeply (cat jump) or scramble over anyhow (fiddle).

It should be explained that, with experience, a rider will be able to recognize whether his horse, when approaching a jump, will arrive within the take-off zone, and to assist him to do so. However, this experience will only come through practice, and, in the first instance, pupils must concentrate upon riding their horses actively forwards, and learning to adapt their own actions and postures to the efforts made by their mounts. They should be told, however, that this is much more than a stopgap measure. There will be numerous occasions throughout their jumping careers when, however skilful they have become, they are unable to reach an obstacle on a good stride. This may be due to some error on their part, to circumstances beyond their control, or simply because a good stride does not exist in the prevailing circumstances.

It is, therefore, essential that riders develop versatility in jumping, but this will happen only if the *instructor* recognizes the importance of versatility. Such recognition will be manifest by a willingness to discuss and explain what happens during different jumps, rather than offering superficial criticism of any action which does not conform to some textbook image. This is not to say that, when dispensing with placing poles, the instructor should not continue to correct jumping errors of those types previously discussed. He should, however, be especially vigilant for problems which are rooted in a pupil's failure to remain in harmony with his horse when he takes off from an indifferent stride, and also to basic riding errors on the approach which contribute towards this happening.

Before proceeding with analysis and explanation, the instructor should ask the pupil for his own assessment. The value of this lies in encouraging pupils to start thinking about whether they are taking off abnormally close to, or far from, a fence, and of the consequent sensations. For the same reason, it is useful for pupils to study each other's jumps, so that they may *see* examples of sensations they have felt themselves. The following points should be considered when the instructor is making his own analysis.

Getting Too Close to a Fence
When a horse gets close to a fence the rider should keep his legs firmly on the horse's sides, and encourage/allow him to pop over in unspectacular fashion. In order to elevate his forehand quickly, the horse will make extra use of forelimbs and shoulders, and the arc of his jump will be relatively steep. The rider will get a sensation of his horse's forehand surging up in front of him, and his vision may be obscured by the horse's neck on the ascent.

Loss of harmony may occur for the following reasons:

1. When the rider anticipates take-off; that is, adopting a forward posture during the approach as previously discussed. The lack of leg contact often associated with this means that the horse has no encouragement to take off when he is having to do so from a point which makes the jump relatively difficult. Furthermore, if the rider's posture is dependent upon his supporting himself on his horse's withers, he will make it harder for the horse to elevate his forehand. Either or both faults will make the jump more hesitant and laboured than necessary, and the rider may become unbalanced either forwards or backwards, depending upon individual circumstances.

2. When the rider is caught out by his horse putting in an extra stride, having thought that he would take off on the previous one. This has some similarities to the above, but results from a momentary misunderstanding rather than from a premeditated, incorrect action. In our context, therefore, it can be considered a much less serious error, although it would have more significance in an established horse/rider partnership jumping larger obstacles.

The element of anticipation and the deceleration as the horse 'puts down' tend to result in the rider tipping forwards rather than folding. Coupled with the typical scrambling jump by the horse, it is unlikely that the result will be a picture of grace and harmony. This is, however, an almost inevitable consequence of the rider being caught out, thus it is fruitless to criticize any but the most serious errors in the jump itself. If he is to be constructive, the instructor should concentrate upon identifying any errors during the approach which may have contributed to the situation arising. The possibilities are:

a. The rider tends to hang on to the reins during the approach, thereby hardening the contact which will cause the horse to jump hollow-backed. If rein contact is hardened during the approach, a horse who is meeting a fence between strides will almost certainly choose to fiddle rather than stand off (if he *does* stand off, he will probably make a very bad jump indeed.) The usual reason for a rider hardening the contact is that he is attempting to control forward movement with the reins alone. In addition to provoking fiddling and a hollow outline, this may cause loss of impulsion, crookedness or even a tendency for the horse to try and rush his fences (through frustration and/or the anticipation of discomfort during the jump). It is, therefore, most important that the pupil be reminded of the principle of controlling a horse by riding 'from leg into hand'. The practical application of this is to establish control with half-halts before starting the approach, and then to ride the horse *forwards*. With a more experienced rider, similar effects may result from his over-checking a horse because he has become preoccupied with looking for a stride – an issue which we shall consider shortly.

b. The rider bustles the horse into a long, flat outline. An enthusiastic rider on a rather lazy horse may well find that speed is easier to obtain than impulsion, and his own keenness may both assist him to sense a long stride and lead him to assume that his horse shares his enthusiasm. The problem is that the horse, hurried out of his rhythm and inevitably on the forehand, finds it easier to put in an extra stride than to make a big effort from a long way out.

Again, the remedy lies in attention to the principles of flatwork. The rider must find means of encouraging impulsion in the horse, rather than continuing to 'row' him along. The usual methods (riding transitions and half-halts) will help in the long term. In the short term (immediately prior to riding the approach) it may help if, instead of relying on increasingly strong leg aids, the rider reinforces light aids with a properly applied whip. Once the horse is more active, the rider should just *maintain* this activity, only increasing leg pressure on the last strides of the approach. If it has become habitual for a pupil to over-ride the approach, a remedial measure is to have him turn relatively short into the fence, rather than to allow him too long a run-up.

3. The rider realizes – perhaps through the horse's hesitation – that he is meeting a fence 'wrong', and assumes that the horse is going to refuse. Because of this assumption, he ceases to support the horse with leg aids, and is unprepared for the horse's effort. Thus the resulting jump – inevitably hesitant and clumsy – causes the rider to become unbalanced backwards. Unfortunately, if not prepared the rider may slip the reins inadequately, or not at all. Although the actual errors at the jump must be pointed out, the instructor should use them to illustrate the wrong thinking which caused them. He should explain that, when riding trained horses over fences well within their capabilities, it should never be *assumed* that they will refuse. Instead, the rider should believe that, given encouragement and opportunity, his horse will always find a way over. By contrast, it must be understood that refusals in such circumstances usually result from lack of opportunity and/or irresolute riding.

Taking off a Long Way From the Fence

When a horse takes off a long way from a fence he has to make an extra powerful effort in order to clear it. This effort creates extra acceleration, giving the rider the sensation of his horse 'attacking' the fence and jumping fast.

A rider is most likely to remain in harmony with such a jump if he realizes the horse's intention, and supports and encourages it. This, however, requires some experience (both general and of the individual horse), and we have already examined the consequences of a rider misreading his mount's intentions in this respect. The opposite – that is, the rider mistakenly believing that the horse would put in another stride before take-off – is the most common cause of loss of harmony when a horse stands off. The result of this is that the rider's weight remains behind the horse's centre of gravity but, if he has genuinely been caught out, this, again, is consequential. There is, therefore, limited value in criticism restricted to the rider's posture – the exception being the matter of slipping the reins. This is something over which the rider does have full control, and it *must* be done in order to prevent the horse from being pulled in the mouth. In this respect, instructors should appreciate that it is not sitting back which is the cardinal error, it is doing so *and not slipping the reins.*

Nevertheless, being caught out in this way does lead a rider to contravene the principle of remaining in harmony, and the causes should be sought by examination of the approach.

We have already seen that, over very small fences, a horse may stand off after losing rhythm and impulsion during the approach, but this becomes less probable as fences get bigger; the horse being more likely to fiddle or refuse. The most prevalent cause of a rider being caught out by his horse's effort is that the horse approaches the fence with a more positive attitude than the rider – in other words the rider is, to some extent, a passenger.

A pupil may fulfil such a role more or less willingly or unwillingly. A willing passenger is quite happy with his horse's way of going, but is too passive; being content to leave everything to the horse, he is insufficiently alert to remain in harmony if the horse makes an abnormal effort. An instructor should explain that, whilst confidence in one's mount is a good thing, a rider should never abdicate his own role; he may, at some stage, ride horses he cannot afford to trust, and he may ride trustworthy horses in circumstances where they require active assistance. Therefore, while he may need to do a minimum of work at present, he should concentrate upon supporting his horse with his legs on the approach and take-off, and giving thought to the likely take-off point. Such advice does not, of course, mean that the pupil will necessarily be able to put his horse right, nor should he, at this stage, be expected to do so. Increased concentration will, however, increase the likelihood of his remaining in harmony with his mount, regardless of where he takes off.

A pupil may be an unwilling passenger if his horse is approaching a fence more strongly than he would wish. We have already touched upon this subject, and the undesirability of riders being carted at jumps, but it is important for instructors to evaluate individual cases on their merits. Novice riders are not infrequently surprised by the way some horses perk up when jumping, and a pupil may approach a fence wishing that he had a little more control, but unwilling to do anything which might interfere with the horse's jump. In such a case, his general attitude is likely to be rather defensive, and he is unlikely to really ask the horse to jump. The instructor can assist with general advice about control; when to be firm (without contravening the principles of correct riding) and when to be subtle with the aids. It may also be appropriate to have the pupil turn fairly short into the fence – perhaps off a circle, or to ride the first part of the approach in a

A pupil may be an unwilling passenger if his horse is approaching a
fence more strongly than he would like

slower gait. Whichever remedies are applied to a particular case, it is essential to remind the pupil of the need to give an aid for take-off; in fact, the more a rider feels his horse is running at a fence, the greater this need becomes, and the firmer the aid should be.

Seeing a Stride

Helping pupils recognize, and adapt to, the different efforts made by their horses incorporates the very first stages of assisting them to see a stride, and it is, therefore, logical to consider this topic at this juncture.

Seeing a stride involves a rider evaluating, during the approach, whether his horse's current stride pattern is going to carry him into the take-off zone. By extension, if it is not, the rider is provided with the time and opportunity to adapt the horse's stride according to his requirements, or, at least, to prepare for the consequences of meeting the fence 'wrong'. Thus the more accurately a rider can see a stride, and the further from the fence he can do so, the greater his chance of a smooth and successful jump.

It will be apparent that some ability to see a stride is essential in any rider with aspirations to jump – especially competitively – beyond novice level, and that it is a considerable benefit for anyone who rides over jumps. However, it is not hard to see that incorrect emphasis upon trying to see a stride can be distracting and disruptive, and some instructors are reluctant to deal with the topic on these grounds. Common objections are that when trying to see a stride, pupils tend to interfere with, rather than assist, their horses, and that not seeing one, or seeing a bad one, provokes negative attitudes. Nevertheless, if an instructor desires to give his pupils a solid grounding in jumping, it will be necessary for him to address this issue, albeit with due care.

In the first instance, he can exercise care in the way he introduces the subject. Declaring, out of the blue, that pupils should be able to tell how many strides they are from a fence, and whether they are going to meet it right is obviously unrealistic and unlikely to inspire confidence. In many cases, however, the introduction is essentially along such lines; an instructor will suddenly announce a lesson on seeing a stride, and expect pupils to count down the last three strides into a fence. Practical objections to this are:

1. It is too big a single learning step.

2. Counting down (to nought) gives a very definite sense of failure if a pupil miscounts his strides, even if the jump itself is perfectly satisfactory.

Although gridwork 'gives' the rider a stride, it also instils a sense of rhythm, which helps when the rider must start looking for his own stride.

3. Riding errors can be provoked by a pupil trying to fit his approach into his counting.

The usual result of such lessons is that pupils gain the impression that the whole concept is beyond them, and the fact that the subject may not be mentioned again for months can lead to their dismissing it completely. Even if they are relatively successful during the lesson, they may view the whole episode as an isolated indulgence of the instructor, which has no real relevance.

What is needed, therefore, is a proper explanation of the value of seeing a stride, and of how the skill is learnt, followed by progressive work towards it in parallel with work on other aspects of jumping. Since we have already dealt with the explanation of the value, we should next consider how to explain that seeing a stride is not the product of some uncanny gift of foresight, but a skill acquired through practice and experience. In order to see a stride, a rider must develop an eye for distance, that is to say, he must learn to evaluate distance in terms relevant to him (his horse's strides in a particular situation), rather than, necessarily, in metres.

This *type* of skill has parallels in many other sports – especially ball games – where it may be accepted, almost unconsciously, both as an integral requirement and one which *all* regular players will, to some extent, acquire. To give examples, all golfers will learn to hit 'touch' shots around the greens with at least a modicum of accuracy and consistency, and all soccer or hockey players will learn to 'weight' their passes so that the majority arrive in the vicinity of the intended recipient. Although some people will prove more adept than others, the common thread is that *all* will improve greatly upon their first attempts, improvement occurring steadily as a result of playing experience and practice.

The lesson to be learnt from this is that everyone can, to some degree, develop an eye for distance – in our context, for a stride – but that development will necessarily be gradual. Acknowledging this should reduce pressure on pupils and instructor alike, and allow the skill to develop naturally as part of overall progress. In practical terms, it will be apparent that the first semblance of seeing a stride will occur not when a pupil is several strides from a fence, but on the last stride before take-off. Therefore, once pupils have some experience of the sensations afforded by horses taking off from different points, they should be asked to nominate how they think they are meeting their fences. This can be done simply by shouting 'close', 'right' or 'long' as appropriate, if and when they think they know. There should be absolutely no pressure on them to nominate their take-off point a particular distance from a fence, nor, at this stage, to try to alter their approach. The instructor should remember that his role is simply to introduce the idea of *thinking* about the approach and that, if they do so consistently, his pupils *will* start to develop an eye for a stride.

If any pupil is experiencing difficulty – or simply to highlight the issue – the instructor can introduce fences which give a prescribed 'feel'. This can be done by building two small doubles, jumpable on both reins, one each side of the arena. Initially, they should provide two even, non-jumping strides, but can then be adjusted in various permutations to ride a little long, a little short, or correct. The adjustment, either way, should be moderate (plus or minus approximately half a metre), and pupils should not be encouraged, as yet, to alter their approaches, but simply to note the different take-off points at the second elements.

I do not feel, at this stage, that there is any great need to emphasize the *number* of strides on the approach, it being more important to a pupil to know how he is meeting a fence than how far he is from it. If, however, an instructor wishes to introduce this issue, I would contend that it is preferable for pupils to count *upwards* during the approach (from a point, within reason, of their choosing), and then to nominate their take-off: 'one, two, three, four, short', 'one, two, long', etc. The value of this is, that since a pupil can keep counting until take-off, he is under no pressure to get the counting 'right', but – provided the counting is not done mindlessly – he will still learn to associate being a certain distance from a fence with a certain number of strides, and this will assist him when he starts to walk courses.

Provided that regular attention is given to the idea of nominating take-off, pupils will find their assessments becoming more accurate, and they will also find that they can assess the take-off whilst somewhat further from the fence. When both factors are occurring regularly, the instructor can introduce the basic principles of adjusting the approach. This must be done with some discretion, and with reference to the abilities shown by both horses and riders to adjust stride length during work on the flat.

He can explain that – as pupils are aware – meeting a fence on an indifferent stride is not necessarily a recipe for disaster. It is, however, obviously better to avoid doing so when possible, and this becomes more significant over bigger obstacles. Therefore, having reached a stage at which they are able to evaluate their approaches, they can start to put their evaluations to practical use.

While it is obviously important for an instructor to give close attention and advice to pupils who are attempting to adjust approaches, the principles can be outlined quite simply.

If a rider sees that his approach is such that the horse is due to take off a longish way from the fence (i.e. just outside the take-off zone), he should ask the horse to lengthen his stride, so that the longer strides carry him to within the take-off zone.

If, however, he realises that his horse would have to take off a very long way from the fence, he should not panic and ride flat out. Although, as a general principle, it is better (and easier) to lengthen into a fence than to shorten, this must be done within the bounds of practicality. Most horses, if badly 'wrong' at a fence, prefer to put in an extra stride and fiddle, and being driven too hard will tend to confuse them. Riders asking for improbably long strides are a major cause of horses 'putting down' clumsily – a situation which can lead to unpleasant accidents.

Therefore, if faced with this situation, it is safer for a rider to allow the extra stride, sitting quietly and supporting the horse with his legs. If sufficiently skilled, he may close his fingers more on the reins, thereby increasing the contact just enough to signal a request for, and acceptance of, the extra stride, without causing interference.

If a rider sees that his horse is due to get rather close to a fence, it is best to accept the situation and proceed as just described. To shorten the stride correctly *during* the approach requires considerable skill and rapport with the horse and, if it is to be done at all, the shortened stride should be established in the early part of the approach. Further to this, if a rider needs to *ensure* that a particular fence is met on a short, bouncy stride, this should be established *before* starting the approach, and then maintained.

If a rider cannot see any sort of stride during the approach, he should neither panic, nor become preoccupied with looking for one. He should simply keep riding forward on an even stride and let the fence come to him. There is a school of thought which suggests that if all approaches are ridden in this way 'there is no such thing as a bad stride'. Although this claim is a considerable exaggeration, the principle still represents the best chance of success if the rider cannot see a stride. It does this by acknowledging that the horse, also, has eyes, and that if he is aimed straight at an obstacle and asked to keep going forwards, he can best comply by jumping. Provided that a horse is generally ridden with competence and consideration, it is amazing how inventive he may be in negotiating an obstacle when 'all the wheels have come off', and this is an excellent reason for encouraging pupils to ride in such a manner. Further to this, it should be remembered that a rider's main object in trying to see a stride is to assist his horse; if he cannot do this, he can at least avoid being a hindrance.

Continuing practice of these principles, as an integral part of jumping lessons, will enable pupils to develop the skill of seeing a stride, and to absorb it naturally into their repertoires. Although the skill will continue to develop, a basic grounding will prove enormously helpful when pupils first venture beyond the confines of the teaching arena.

CHAPTER 9

Towards More Variety

Once pupils have developed the basic skills of jumping over fences of straightforward design, the instructor can start introducing more variety; of fences, of approaches and of horses. Although the long-term aim of this is to prepare pupils for competitive jumping, there is considerable value purely within the context of lessons, since this variety will stimulate interest, teach pupils to really think about what they are jumping, and promote accurate, disciplined riding. As with all teaching, however, the instructor should take care not to introduce too many new ideas at once; they should be introduced gradually so that they can be fully absorbed.

Fences

Having started jumping over fences which slope a little away from the direction of approach, pupils should next be introduced to both uprights and significantly-sloping spreads (triple bars, etc.). Although each of these types represents just one step away from the design of the introductory fences, their contrasting appearances will highlight the fact that obstacles can vary considerably, and that they need to be considered as individual constructions rather than just jumps.

The different characteristics of these fences should be explained to the pupils. They should be told that upright fences are less inviting to a horse than those with a little slope and spread, and require greater accuracy. The lack of contour means that a horse who stands off is more likely to flatten and hit an upright, and a horse who gets close to the groundline has less room to elevate when he tries to fiddle. The redeeming feature, however, is that being in a single plane, they are comparatively easy for a rider to 'measure'.

By contrast, a triple bar presents a very inviting aspect to a horse, but may confuse an inexperienced rider. Pupils may find, initially, that they are asking/expecting their horse to take off further from such fences than is necessary, or else thinking that they have got too close, only to find that this is not the case. When this happens, it will be because pupils are measuring the fence from the front pole rather than the highest point, and this is a good reason to encourage them to look forwards rather than down.

As a basic type of fence, true parallels should be introduced last of all. They always look bigger than they measure, and require a greater physical effort to jump than other designs of the same height – thus increasing the need for an active and accurate approach. However despite, or because of, this, they should definitely *be* introduced because it would be bad teaching practice to let pupils face a challenge for the first time when outside the teacher's sphere of influence. Furthermore, a parallel which is quite low but relatively wide can be used to give pupils the 'feel' of quite a big jump, and will make a good warm up jump before larger fences of a different design are taken. A parallel should have only a single pole on the far side.

Once introduced, these various types of fences can be incorporated into combinations. At first, it is good practice to use an inviting spread as a first element, and a simple upright as a last element. This is because, while a sloping spread will encourage a bold jump into a combination, a spread as a final element can be rather demanding if any loss of impulsion and stride pattern occurs.

In addition to varying the types of element in a combination, the number of elements and the stride intervals can also now be varied; simple trebles and bounce fences being introduced. At first, unless the elements are very small, trebles should not have two single stride intervals – there should be two strides between the second and third elements, and all elements should be of a straightforward design.

Bounce fences must be introduced with care. It is important to explain what takes place during a bounce and, in particular, to emphasize the need to give a take-off aid for the second element as well as the first. The instructor must also ensure that the distance between elements is appropriate to circumstances; this requires care, since the potential for variation in a bounce is proportionately greater than in a combination containing non-jumping strides – and there is less room for adjustment. By way of guidance, appropriate bounce distances when jumping from trot will range from approximately 2.75 metres for a small, short-striding animal to approximately 3.5 metres for a longer-striding horse. When jumping from canter, distances should be increased on a sliding scale by between approximately

0.5 metres and 1 metre. (Course builders, especially of solid fences, should note that the total range – from approximately 2.75 metres to 4.5 metres – dictates that it is impractical to provide one set-distance bounce to cater for a cross-section of competitors, and that attempting to do so is highly dangerous.)

Since jumping bounce fences successfully requires controlled impulsion, and lack of control is potentially dangerous, an instructor should not encourage/allow a pupil to take a bounce if his horse is getting away from him. It makes sense, in fact, to introduce pupils to bounce fences by having them take small elements from trot, the approach being regulated by trotting poles. Similarly, when first jumping bounces from canter, a fairly short approach and a placing pole should be employed.

Bounces can be usefully employed at the start of combinations and, in due course, double bounces can be used by themselves to encourage pupils in the maintenance and control of their horses' energy. Bounce distances should not, however, be incorporated into combinations so as to follow intervals containing non-jumping strides, since they will compound any difficulties engendered earlier in the combination.

Once pupils are accustomed to the different types of fence, it is worthwhile including the occasional obstacle with unusual characteristics. By using

Do not encourage a pupil to take a bounce if the horse is getting away from him

the term 'unusual', I am not suggesting that obstacles should be off-putting or unsuitable for the horses, but simply that the materials and con-struction should be novel to the riders. The purpose of this is both to provide an intro-duction to some of the specific 'oddities' they may meet in the future, and to stimulate their abilities to analyse obstacles *in the horse's terms*. This, hopeful-ly, will prevent their making either of two common errors:

1. Riding fussily or without commitment at a fence because, by applying *human* criteria, they have convinced themselves that the *horse* will dislike it. An example of this might be a fence incorporating novelty fillers in the shape of some animal. The rider will think 'my horse will never jump those sheep/pigs/cows' whereas, in all probability, the horse will not even recognise the representations.

2. Riding carelessly at a fence because they have not appreciated a factor which increases the difficulty in equine terms. Whilst an instructor of novices must be very careful about providing fences which are difficult for horses, a simple example would be a narrow fence without wings, where careless riding might encourage a horse to take the soft option of running out.

Examples of unusual materials which can be usefully employed include: the more oddly painted and designed poles, planks and fillers, marker cones and straw bales, but *not* tyres laid flat, anything hard to see, highly reflective, mobile or audible. Examples of unusual constructions include: uprights with poles not horizontal (i.e. cups on one wing a couple of holes higher than the other), 'fans' (a single wing one side, and two or more on the other, the poles arranged as an upright on the single wing and a spread on the other side), stiles, and other low, narrow-faced fences without wings, but *not* anything with a false groundline.

The crux of instructing pupils jumping unusual fences is to convince them that, regardless of whether their concern is about their own or their horses' reactions, they should neither charge such fences flat out and shrieking, nor should they give up the moment they receive a negative signal from the horse. They should, rather, adhere to the basic principles of jumping and ride firm, controlled approaches, offering calm verbal *reassurance* as appropriate.

Approaches

Mention of controlled approaches brings us to consideration of variety in this area. In the early stages, when the emphasis is upon improving technique and confidence in the act of jumping, approaches should be as straightforward as possible in all respects. As pupils progress, however, it is useful and necessary to instil the ability to present a horse straight and going forward at a fence despite the various approaches which may appear in the show ring or across country.

Work on controlled approaches should place emphasis upon both gait and direction. Some thoughts (which should be conveyed to the pupils) and exercises which may prove useful are:

Approaches from Walk

There are times, especially in cross-country riding, when it may be necessary to ride most of an approach in walk, and this can also be useful in setting up a difficult horse to jump a very narrow obstacle. Approaches in walk can either be ridden round a fairly tight turn, with enough room after the turn for three strides of trot, or they can be straight, with pupils asking for trot at a predetermined point. It is essential that the walk be active, pupils being reminded of the quality of gait required for a *good* upward transition on the flat; harsh or flustered aids to trot and jump will probably indicate deficiencies in the walk. Fences must necessarily be low but, if pupils prove adept, they need not remain *very* low; it being useful for pupils to appreciate the potential for jumping significant obstacles in this manner. These exercises should be performed sparingly, in order that horses do not start to anticipate; this would not only be undesirable in principle, but would also impair the emphasis upon control.

Approaches from Trot

Trot can be a very useful gait when jumping, especially on inexperienced, unbalanced or difficult horses, or when the terrain/siting is not favourable to approaching in canter. Trotting often promotes better balance and control than canter, allows horse and rider more time, and has the effect of creating more room – a trot stride covering less ground than a canter stride. There are many exercises which can be performed in trot but, if a horse keeps jumping from trot round the arena perimeter he may start offering canter before or after each jump, and this may cause the rider to start hanging on to him. It is better, therefore, to perform exercises which include frequent changes of rein/direction, this, in itself, being beneficial to pupils. Examples include figures of eight (with variations) over fences set across the long diagonals, two-loop serpentines over fences set along the centre line, and the clover leaf, over fences set in cross formation around the centre of the

Exercises in approaching fences

Approaches in walk, trotting (dotted line) at predetermined point

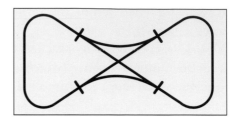

Approaching in trot: figure of eight with variations

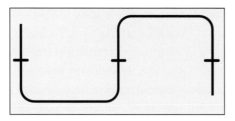

Approaching in trot: two-loop serpentine

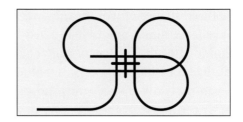

Approaching in trot: clover leaf

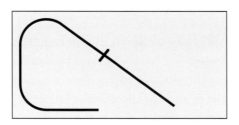

Approaching in canter: turning across long diagonal

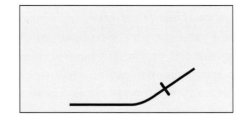

Approaching in canter: fence offset from arena side

arena. With the accent being on control and accuracy, fences should be kept low (approximately 0.5 metres).

Approaches from Canter

Since canter is the gait most frequently used for jumping, it is important that pupils refine their abilities to approach fences in this gait. However, it is also important – and often overlooked – to realise that there is no logic in attempting movements in canter *over fences* which horses/riders are unable to perform satisfactorily *on the flat*. The two obvious examples of this are tight turns and flying changes. Therefore, until pupils reach such proficiency, the accent should be on accuracy rather than tightness of turns, and changes of canter lead should be made through trot. Useful exercises include turning to jump fences on the long diagonals, and turning to jump fences offset from the long sides of the arena. The clover leaf exercise mentioned above is valuable, but requires a teaching area at least 30 metres wide if novices are to perform it in canter.

Horses

Within the bounds of common sense, it is good experience for pupils to jump a greater variety of horses as they progress. Horses should occasionally be swopped as appropriate during lessons and, as pupils become more confident and proficient, slightly more demanding animals can be introduced.

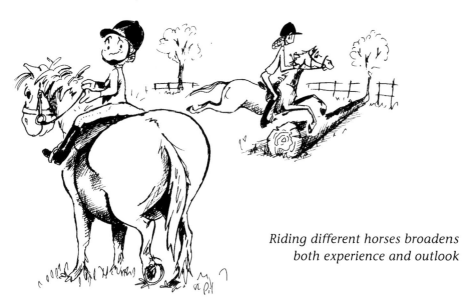

Riding different horses broadens both experience and outlook

Riding different horses is always valuable and instructive; it broadens both experience and outlook, making riders more adaptable and effective. Within the context of jumping, pupils should be encouraged to note factors such as how different shapes and sizes of horses (and saddles) can affect optimum length of stirrup leathers, how horses' attitudes and responses vary during the approach to a fence, and differences in stride lengths. Such information will be particularly useful to non-owner riders who may start competitive jumping on a variety of unfamiliar hired horses.

CHAPTER 10

CROSS-COUNTRY JUMPING

IF AN INSTRUCTOR is really to teach jumping, the teaching process must necessarily include instruction in jumping solid obstacles across country. The reason for this is that, in the majority of equestrian sports where jumping is a factor, this is the type of jumping required. While the general principles of riding and jumping will apply in any environment, it will be apparent that there are various factors pertaining to cross-country jumping which will not be encountered in a teaching arena. The crux of teaching cross-country jumping is, therefore, to broaden pupils understanding and experience in order that they can deal with these factors.

The Transition to Riding in the Open

We have seen that, when teaching jumping in an arena, it is an essential pre-requisite that pupils can ride fairly proficiently on the flat. Since we are considering cross-country instruction only for pupils who have already learnt the basics of jumping in an arena, it might seem that the question of riding proficiency would no longer arise. This, however, may not be the case.

The ability to ride on the flat in an arena is not entirely the same as the ability to do so across country, and it is by no means uncommon to encounter people who are quite proficient at the former, but have little or no experience of the latter. An additional consideration is that, even if pupils do have quite a lot of experience of hacking, they may have actually *learnt* very little about riding in the open. Hacking, too often, is either pony trekking under a posher name, or a disorganised scramble escorted by someone whose knowledge and skill are hardly greater than those being escorted; the old idea of continuing the teaching process when riding out appears to be on the decline.

Given this state of affairs, the instructor teaching cross-country jumping must be prepared also to give instruction in cross-country riding. Although this is not the main province of this book, it may be worth giving consideration to some major points.

General Control

It is quite usual for horses to show rather more sparkle out in the open than within the confines of the arena. However, for a rider who has not previously experienced this, it may come as quite a shock if a horse he has been riding quite competently in the school appears to undergo a character transformation, and suddenly pays scant attention to his aids. This will be compounded by the fact that he is riding in the open, away from the constraints of the arena perimeter.

Riders can react to this 'culture shock' in various ways but, unassisted, it is likely that their reactions will be rooted in loss of confidence, and will engender riding errors. The instructor's task, therefore, is firstly to prepare pupils mentally for the transition, and secondly, to explain how to adapt their riding in order that they retain effective control.

In the first instance, pupils should be told that the move into a more natural environment from one which they associate mainly with work *is* likely to make horses perk up, and that cross-country riders should consider this an asset. It should be explained that, to perform well across country, a horse must be reasonably fit (one of the manifestations of which is enthusiasm) and reasonably free-going (because riding a sluggish/reluctant horse across country is very hard work indeed, and jumping solid obstacles on such a mount is not much fun). These assets will, of course, be more appreciated by riders if they are able to utilise them rather than becoming victims of them, and this brings us to the consideration of pupils' understanding of aid applications, and the postural adaptations which can assist control.

Aids

Pupils should be reminded that although it is a principle of equitation that aids should be applied as lightly *as is effective*, the fundamental purpose of an aid is to achieve the desired response. To this end, aid applications have to be varied according to circumstance. If a horse is a little excited and/or preoccupied with his surroundings, it may well be necessary to apply certain aids more firmly than if he were calm and attentive. This is especially true when riding at the faster gaits in the open, when lack of effective control is a

Rider wearing a body protector
and crash hat. Both are now
mandatory for many cross-country
competitions.

Below: Cantering in the open.
Riders must be confident and in
control before they can start
cross-country jumping.

potential source of danger to rider, horse and bystanders. In this environment, it may help pupils with a tendency to diffidence if they think in terms of 'telling' rather than 'asking' their horses. This is not to suggest that aid applications should ever be fundamentally incorrect or unnecessarily harsh; indeed the purpose of explanation and preparation is that they are likely to prevent, rather than induce, abuses resulting from shock reactions.

Posture

We have already touched upon the principles of adaptation for cross-country riding whilst considering adaptations for jumping, but it remains most important to ensure that pupils are aware of the existence of both the centres of gravity and motion, the differences between them and the effects of placing their weight over each. From their experiences of jumping they should, of course, be fully familiar with those influences relating to the centre of gravity, but it may be necessary to explain those relating to the centre of motion in detail, and also how a restraining posture can be used in conjunction with a steady contact on one rein and a check and release contact on the other to retain control of a horse who is becoming stronger than desired. It may, in fact, be a good idea to demonstrate this, both because this is surprisingly rarely done, and in order that pupils are not misled into sawing or jabbing actions of the reins. Since riding with shortened stirrup leathers will facilitate placing the weight over the horse's centre of gravity, increase the effectiveness of the restraining posture and lessen the chances of losing a stirrup when riding over rough or unlevel ground, pupils should keep their leathers at jumping length for cross-country work, regardless of whether or not they are actually jumping.

Dealing with Natural Terrain

Riding up, down and across slopes, and coping with less than perfect ground conditions must become integral parts of a cross-country rider's art, and he will often have to jump whilst performing these feats. While it is not suggested that pupils need to be comprehensively versed in all these matters before doing any cross-country jumping, it is certainly necessary for them to be familiar with specific conditions before being expected to jump *where such conditions prevail*.

Riding up and down hill have much in common with the ascent and descent phases of jumping, and the instructor can draw useful parallels, especially regarding the desirability of riders remaining in dynamic balance with their mounts. However, since riding up or down a slope will take a good deal longer than jumping, pupils will have more time to feel whether or not they *are* in balance, and an instructor will have more time to assess and correct any errors. It may, indeed, be instructive to both parties to see whether tendencies towards persistent jumping errors are mirrored when riding up and down hill.

The main difference between riding hills and jumping is that, with the former, there is often an option just to ascend or descend. This is significant because, although the principles (remaining in harmony, retaining control through sympathetic leg and rein contact) are the same for both they are much easier to adhere to when ascending. The reasons for this should be explained to pupils in conjunction with instruction as to *how* to deal with the consequences.

Riding Uphill

Because a horse's source of locomotive power is in his hind limbs, it is well placed to propel him uphill; although he will expend more energy moving uphill than on level ground, the process is relatively easy in mechanical terms – certainly easier than moving down or across a slope. The rider's role is to ensure that the hindquarters are unencumbered and that their load is as stable and compact as possible, and he will achieve this by keeping his own weight as close to the horse's centre of gravity as possible. It will be instructive for pupils to note that the horse's need to really use his hindquarters, coupled with his carrying his head and neck quite low as an aid to balance, will put him into a 'rounded' outline. The rider should not interfere with this outline by bustling the horse out of his rhythm, nor by pulling on the reins should the horse try to hurry of his own volition; in the latter case, quite light, correctly applied aids, coupled with the prospect of expending extra energy, should be sufficient to dissuade the horse from rushing. Once pupils can apply these principles correctly up lesser slopes in the slower gaits, there is no reason why they should not progress quite swiftly to steeper slopes and faster gaits.

Downhill Control

Going downhill in a measured, balanced fashion is relatively difficult for a horse, since he has to contend both with the effects of gravity and the fact that his source of locomotive power is higher up the slope than the rest of his body. If he does not make efforts to regulate his movement, his progress will be unbalanced and hurried. Furthermore, if he does not move as straight down the slope as possible, he will aggravate the natural tendency for his hindquarters to try and overtake his forehand, with the result that he may slip sideways or even fall.

There are several points to be considered if pupils are to assist, rather than impede their horses when riding downhill. Firstly, they must not be tense and nervous; such conditions, relayed to a horse via a stiff, tight seat, fiercely gripping legs and heavy rein contact, will upset him both mentally and physically. Specific problems are the reluctance of a nervous rider to allow his horse to adopt a low head carriage for fear of having nothing in front of him, and the probability of such a rider attempting to tug his horse up with the reins should he suffer loss of balance. (With regard to these errors, pupils must be told that, if a horse *does* slip or stumble, they must sit still and *allow* him all the rein he requires to recover, and that pulling at a horse's head while he is travelling downhill is counter-productive at best, and a recipe for potential disaster.)

Obviously, ensuring lack of tension in pupils is a responsibility of the instructor, who must be sure to introduce riding downhill with care. He must start with short, gentle slopes ridden in walk, progressing to longer, steeper slopes at the same gait before expecting pupils to negotiate significant slopes at faster gaits. Furthermore, before the matter of riding downhill at faster gaits is addressed, pupils must first have demonstrated their abilities to control the same mounts at these gaits on level ground.

The next consideration is that pupils are made aware of the need to establish the required gait and gait quality *before* starting a descent. Since it takes sympathetic and intelligent riding to *retain* gait quality downhill, there is little likelihood of improving a gait once the descent has started. A rider who lacks control at the outset is simply likely to lose it further, which is not only undesirable in itself, but also because attempts to regain control may well give rise to serious riding errors. During the descent itself, pupils should sit still and do nothing to provoke loss of straightness in their horses. As with jumping, there is no specific position for riding downhill; the correct posture being that which keeps the rider in balance with his horse. The instructor should dissuade pupils from adopting extreme, arbitrary postures. Leaning right back with legs rammed forward is unhelpful to the horse and – except in a real emergency – unnecessary for the rider. On the other hand, leaning forwards with some vague intention of unburdening the hindquarters but without reference to the horse's movement may simply result in the rider overburdening the horse's forehand and imperilling his own security.

Riding Across Slopes

Moving across a slope is not particularly easy for a horse, for the simple reason that all his legs are the same length. In order to retain his equilibrium he will have to make adjustments to his movement, and his gaits will inevitably be affected to some degree. He will also have a natural tendency to drift downhill. If a rider is to minimise these effects he should firstly, given choice of route, traverse the least steep part of a slope along the shortest possible line. He should sit erect and, if necessary, keep his downhill leg on the girth rather more firmly than usual, to counteract any drift. If cantering, it is preferable for the horse to be leading with his uphill (fore)leg since this, too, will help counteract drift. In general, gait and speed should be adjusted as little as possible.

Imperfect Going

Although instructors should not expect inexperienced pupils to ride – let alone jump – on very bad going, they may well have little control over the ground upon which they teach, and they obviously have none at all over the weather. Teaching pupils to cope with imperfect going may, therefore, be immediately necessary as well as providing preparation for the future.

Before dealing with specific examples, an instructor should emphasize that, by definition, any form of bad going will be a hindrance to horses, and will increase the risk of physical damage. Riders should, therefore, always try to find the best going available, and should remain constantly sensitive to their horses movements.

The types of bad going most usually encountered can be divided broadly into hard, slippery and heavy. A horse who is 'feeling' hard ground will be reluctant to stride out, and will move gingerly. Under such circumstances, the rider should not attempt to bustle him along (which will do more harm than good), but should apply just sufficient leg aids to maintain an acceptable degree of forward movement. If it is necessary to jump under such circumstances, the rider should give firm aids, but must not expect the horse to lengthen his stride into a fence, nor to stand off.

On slippery going, a rider must sit very still, apply the aids as lightly as possible, and in good time, and be constantly prepared to slip the reins. Any jumps must be approached steadily, in the slowest gait practical, and the horse should be allowed to just pop over.

Heavy 'sticky' going is both difficult and tiring to move through, and some horses lose their action and wallow through it; problems which will be compounded by an unstable, interfering rider. A rider should, therefore sit well over the horse's centre of motion, keep a light contact on a good length of rein, and use his legs sufficiently to support, but not hurry, the horse. Bearing in mind that jumping out of such ground requires considerable extra effort, he should ensure that impulsion is maintained throughout the approach, and give a firm aid for take-off. Again, horses should not be asked or expected to stand off fences out of such going.

Jumping

The additional factors to be considered when making the transition from jumping in an arena to jumping cross-country are:

1. Cross-country obstacles are usually solid.

2. In some instances, natural obstacles may be more awkwardly sited than in a show jumping course.

3. On *average*, they will be taken faster than in an arena – although this does not, and should not, necessarily apply to each individual obstacle.

4. Where obstacles are taken faster, a horse's stride on the approach will generally be longer than would be normal in an arena.

5. Stride length may be modified by variations in terrain and ground conditions across country.

6. Variations in terrain will also affect the flight of a horse's jump.

An instructor must, therefore, devise a teaching programme which will expand his pupils abilities to deal with these factors.

Pupils must first be introduced to the idea of jumping solid fences. As with jumping in general, this is an issue which may arouse a variety of responses; some pupils think nothing of it and others find the prospect of knock-down poles being substituted by solid fences daunting initially. The instructor should pre-empt any concern by explaining that solid, readily-visible obstacles are about the easiest a horse can be asked to jump, since it will be obvious to him that they *are* obstacles, and that they need jumping cleanly.

The best way to convince pupils of the truth of this is, of course, through their personal experience, and instilling confidence must be an instructor's priority. To this end, first cross-country fences should be sited on good, level ground, be low (approximately 0.6 metres) but solid and imposing, and present a good wide face (4 metres or so). The presence of at least one natural wing (e.g. a field boundary fence) is also helpful at an early stage. Pupils should jump such fences from canter towards, but not directly at, the other horses. They should be reminded to observe the basic principles as applied in the school; in particular, the need to ride into the fence and give an aid for take-off.

Once initial confidence is established, some time should be spent on consolidation; jumping a selection of similar fences, with somewhat bigger obstacles gradually being introduced. If possible, half a dozen or so should be combined into a miniature course, preferably round a single field in plain view, the emphasis being on jumping from a good, even canter.

The next stage is to emphasize the practical importance of maintaining control and impulsion and making room when tackling awkwardly sited obstacles. Since the main concern here is the approach, and pupils may make initial errors, the obstacles themselves should be either low (small fallen trees) or capable of dislodgement (piles of brushwood). They must, however, still be recognisable as jumps; miniature piles of assorted debris will simply encourage carelessness. The most helpful environment for this type

Tackling a solid obstacle at home. The rider's leathers are a little too long, and her lower leg position is not very secure, but she is going nicely 'with' her horse, and allowing him to stretch his neck.

of work is an area of woodland which has been reconnoitred by the instructor. Useful exercises include: weaving through the undergrowth at walk to jump an obstacle from three or four strides of trot (promotes maintenance of impulsion); taking one or two jumps along a major track and then turning down a minor track to take another (promotes maintenance of control); taking a jump sited just round the inside corner of a wide track (emphasizes the need to make room).

By now, pupils should be feeling at home in the outdoor environment, and increasingly confident with both riding and jumping. This being the case, emphasis can be placed on jumping at greater speed. While some instructors might baulk at this prospect, the fact is that those who ride across country are, sooner or later, going to do so quickly, and they will do so better, and more safely, if they have been taught how.

The fast work should be done on good going, and in a location where there is plenty of room to slow down gradually and safely. Ideally, the fences should be located in a broad, sweeping curve (for instance, round three sides

Only through correct, sound instruction will the rider gain the skill and confidence to school novice horses over solid obstacles.

of a large field). Although the ground should be reasonably level, the route must run up, rather than down, any slight incline. Such a layout will tend to aid control and there is the additional bonus that, once each pupil has finished, he can return to the rest of the ride so that horses waiting their turn are not tempted to rush off toward distant companions. The fences themselves must be straightforward and inviting: single elements with some degree of slope away from the direction of approach.

When teaching jumping at speed, an instructor must give extra consideration to control both between, and at, the fences. While we have just dealt with the former in general terms, it should be emphasized that, when travelling at speed, it is more important than ever to have the horse on the aids. This will be signified by his moving freely forwards into his rider's hands, neither taking an unduly strong contact nor needing to be ridden along with repeated leg aids. A rider will not achieve this by abandoning the rein contact and giving his horse a boot in the ribs, nor by unnecessarily harsh restraint; the latter, in fact, merely destroys the horse's rhythm and *provokes* resistances (encouraging the horse to pull and fight for his head).

Pupils should, rather, be encouraged to ride proper, progressive transitions through trot to canter, gradually allowing their horses to lengthen stride and quicken until the required gait and speed are established. Once this is achieved, they can remain in a poised posture over, or just behind, the horse's centre of gravity. Should it become necessary to exercise restraint, or urge the horse forward, a rider can move his weight back over the horse's centre of motion and apply the appropriate aids. With regard to the actual process of jumping, it is when travelling at speed in a poised posture that riders are most likely to be tempted to remain in such a posture throughout the approach. It is, therefore, essential that pupils be reminded to sit and apply their legs on the final strides of approach; by doing so, they can avoid trotting out the oldest 'sucker' line in jumping – 'he was going so well I felt sure he would just jump it'.

The other point to bring to the pupils' attention is that horses moving at speed, with long strides, will find it easier to stand off than fiddle if they meet a fence between strides; also, they may stand off a little further than they might in the school. If, however, a horse *does* fiddle in these circumstances, the change of stride length and deceleration will be more marked than usual, resulting in a distinctly proppy jump off the forehand; another reason why riders should not over-commit themselves.

Once pupils are jumping satisfactorily on fairly level ground, work can begin on jumping up, down and across slopes. Since jumping across slopes is the odd one out of these disciplines and requires the least explanation, we should perhaps deal with it first. If pupils are to jump a fence so sited, they should approach it somewhat uphill (commensurate with meeting it at a reasonable angle), and should favour aiming for the uphill half of the fence.

Tackling fences up and down slopes calls for consideration of various factors, of which pupils must be made aware. When approaching a fence uphill, a horse's stride will be shorter than on level ground, his hind limbs will (it is hoped) be actively engaged, and his body will be inclined upwards (broadly parallel to the slope). Although he will be expending more energy than when moving on level ground these factors can otherwise be considered generally helpful to the act of jumping. However, a consequence of the uphill approach is that the take-off point is lower than the base of the fence, which will therefore require a bigger effort to clear than if it were sited on level ground. This state of affairs can be complicated by the fact that, since course-builders measure the height of a fence from its likely take-off point, a fence sited uphill measured at 0.9 metres – and requiring commensurate effort to jump – may actually be only 0.7 metres high. It will, therefore *look* smaller than it jumps, a situation which can induce carelessness in both horse and rider. The final consideration of jumping a fence uphill is that, while the arc of the jump will begin more steeply than from level ground, it will also finish earlier, the horse landing into the slope and deceleration being more marked than usual.

A rider can take account of these factors by:

1. Taking off from the edge of the take-off zone nearer to the fence, thus decreasing its effective height.

2. Imagining that the fence is rather higher than it looks, and riding it somewhat more strongly than might seem necessary, thereby reducing the possibility of carelessness.

3. Placing his weight well over the horse's centre of gravity on take-off, but not 'holding' the posture so long as to be rocked forward on landing.

When approaching a fence downhill, a horse's stride will be longer than on level ground, it will be harder for him to engage his hind limbs, and his body will be inclined downwards. Although he will be expending less energy in generating forward movement, he will have to make extra effort to maintain his balance. The downhill approach will result in the take-off point being higher than the base of the fence, thus reducing its effective height. Jumping from the optimum take-off point will, therefore, require less effort than jumping a similar fence on level ground. However, the increase in stride length increases the chance of meeting a fence between strides, in which case a horse may stand off abnormally far, thus needing to elevate very little, but having to make a considerable jump forwards. Alternatively, if he gets close to the fence, he will increase its effective height and have to make a considerable effort to get off his forehand to clear it. Because the arc of the jump will finish later than on level ground, the horse will land more steeply.

A rider must bear in mind the importance of not interfering with a horse when travelling downhill; in general this will mean not trying too hard to ride onto a stride, but simply supporting the horse with the legs and waiting for the jump. When faced with the choice, horses tend to favour standing off downhill fences, but they should not be given over-vigorous encouragement to do so, since this may unbalance them and cause them to dive over the fence, landing nose first. If a horse does stand off, and over downhill fences in general, a rider must be prepared to slip his reins, for their mutual benefit. This may, in fact, be *necessitated* by the steepness of the landing; if a rider is to keep his weight over (and not in front of) the horse's centre of gravity he will, in the latter stages of the jump, have to unfold his upper body to a greater degree than usual, either straightening his arms or slipping the reins to avoid pulling his horse in the mouth.

This leads us to the consideration of drop fences. While any fence taken downhill incorporates an element of 'drop', specifically designed drop fences usually have a marked variation in levels between the take-off and landing sides, and this increases the steepness of the last part of the jumping arc. It is, therefore, prudent for pupils to have some experience of jumping downhill before being introduced to such obstacles.

The key to jumping drops successfully is for the rider to adapt to the steepness of landing, and to the consequential effects of deceleration. He can do this by remaining a little behind the horse's centre of gravity during the descent, the simplest way to achieve this being to assume a vertical upper body posture once the horse has passed the highest point of his jumping arc. With his upper body upright, and the descent steep, it becomes rather unnatural for a rider to keep his legs on the girth, and such a position will do little to absorb the shock of landing. Therefore, while pupils should not be encouraged to ram their legs forward (which will just lock knee and ankle joints and push them up out of the saddle on landing), there is no need to fight a natural tendency for legs to swing forward so that the ankle joints are vertically beneath hips and shoulders. It will be noted, in fact, that such a

Solid lines show actual height of fence (same in both cases). Dotted lines 'A' show effective height of fence jumped from far edge of take-off zone. Dotted lines 'B' show effective height of fence jumped from near edge of take-off zone . (Course-builders' measured heights would correspond approximately to 'B' heights.)

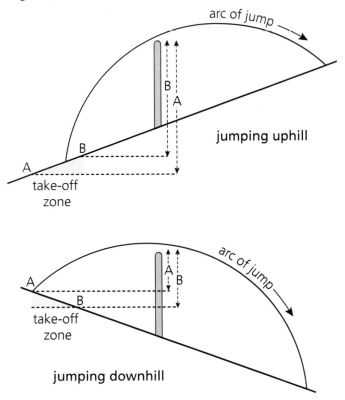

The geometry of jumping on slopes

posture corresponds closely to a normal posture on the flat, and that the rider is not actually leaning back at all.

The best way to introduce pupils to drops is by using a simple step down, so that the drop element comprises the whole jump. In this way, pupils can concentrate upon their posture, and gain confidence in coping with the drop. Once this is achieved, they can be introduced gradually to various obstacles incorporating fence and drop together.

In addition to the elements so far discussed, there are two types of obstacle which merit special consideration, since they have inherent features which affect their jumping characteristics. They are water and ditches. When introducing these obstacles, care should be taken to ensure that all take-off and landing points are safe, and that the bottom of any stretch of water gives a secure footing. As with other types of obstacle, it is important that pupils are mounted on horses who are known to take them confidently.

Since jumping *over* water is much the same as jumping a dry ditch, let us consider the water obstacles that have to be jumped into, through or out of. The special feature of water is the braking effect it exerts, which increases the landing deceleration of a jump into it, and slows down a horse moving through it. Before they attempt jumping into or out of water it is, therefore, good policy for pupils to experience this braking effect by simply riding through it. Noting the effect upon their horses speed and stride length, they should concentrate upon retaining active movement without bustling their horses; indeed, parallels can be drawn with riding through heavy going.

The next step is for pupils to jump small solid fences out of shallow water onto fairly level ground; they should be advised that the braking effect makes it inappropriate to concentrate much upon trying to ride strides, and that they should keep their horses going forward and wait for the jump.

Having jumped out of water satisfactorily, pupils can then tackle jumping into it. Since this inevitably entails some degree of drop it is logical, as with other drop fences, for the first jump to consist simply of a step from a low bank into shallow water. Pupils should employ the same criteria as for a normal drop, but must be especially careful to allow the horse to have freedom of his head.

One feature of a simple step into water is that it permits a very steady approach. It is generally reckoned that the best way to jump into water is as slowly as possible, but this rule should perhaps be expanded by including the phrase 'commensurate with retaining enough impulsion for a smooth jump'. Even when just stepping off a low bank, horse and rider will retain their balance more readily if the process is a smooth one, and pupils must neither encourage nor cause their horses to dither on the brink. This consideration assumes greater importance still when riders reach the stage of jumping over a fence into water; although they *do* want to enter as slowly as possible, they *must* have sufficient impulsion to jump the fence cleanly – a horse who scrambles over (or hits) a fence into water is very likely to topple over on landing.

Jumping a significant fence into water does, in fact, require considerable skill and a co-operative horse, and thus pupils should have a good deal of practice over very low fences into water of moderate depth and over modest fences into very shallow water before greater demands are made of them. Similarly, jumping a combination obstacle through water should not be attempted until pupils have consistently demonstrated balance and control over single elements.

The special feature of ditches is that horses tend to have an instinctive distrust of holes in the ground, and thus even those who can be relied upon to jump ditches may have a good look at them first, and jump unexpectedly high. While an instructor must apprise pupils of these realities, he must avoid doing so in a manner which invokes trepidation or desperation. Trepidation will result in a rider dithering up to a ditch half expecting a refusal, thereby persuading his horse that it is full of nameless horrors, and getting the expected result. Desperation will result in a flat-out approach in the hope that 'by the time the horse sees the ditch he will be going too fast to stop'; a formula most likely to result in rider and/or horse ending up in the bottom. Such attitudes being clearly unsatisfactory, the instructor's aim must be to engender *respect* for ditches, and a determined attitude, with pupils riding strong, controlled approaches. It will help to achieve this if pupils and horses are warmed-up and jumping confidently before tackling ditches which should, therefore, be introduced in the latter stages of a lesson. The first part of the lesson should consist of jumping easy, familiar obstacles, moving on to larger fences of imposing appearance but straight-forward construction: log piles, sleepers, etc. Though pupils should not be jumping these fences for the first time, their nature is such as to promote the type of approach required for ditches. If, therefore, a pupil jumps a couple of these immediately prior to tackling his first ditch, and is told to ride the ditch just as he has ridden the preceding fences, this should put him on the right lines.

(It should be noted that natural ditches with crumbling or otherwise treacherous banks have to be ridden with greater caution, usually from a slow approach and with regard to individual circumstances. Such obstacles should *not*, however, be used for novice instruction.)

CHAPTER 11

FALLS

ALTHOUGH ONE purpose of this book is to promote safe instruction, it would be unrealistic to suggest that any jumping instructor could guarantee that none of his pupils would ever fall. This is because, however safe their teaching, no-one has absolute control over horses, riders or extraneous circumstances.

Falls can be broadly divided into three categories:

1. Those where serious injury (demanding professional treatment) is sustained

Such falls are, mercifully, quite rare, but their possible occurrence cannot be dismissed. It is therefore essential, as a minimum requirement, that instructors are familiar with basic accident procedures such as those outlined in the Association of British Riding Schools Accident Procedure (see page 116). The main purpose of such knowledge is not that it equips its possessor to replace a qualified professional, but that it equips him to deal with the immediate situation, summon assistance and convey relevant information with optimum efficiency.

More detailed knowledge of first aid is obviously advantageous, but it is important not to attempt procedures and treatments beyond one's real competence since mistakes can, in certain circumstances, have tragic results. (In this respect, if a person is unconscious, or unable to move fingers or toes, they MUST NOT be moved, except by properly equipped professionals. In the event of a suspected head injury, the hat MUST NOT be removed.)

Further to this theme it is useful (not just in the context of jumping) for stables to have a note of any client's medical condition which may require special consideration in the event of an accident; such information should, however, be sought with considerable tact.

2. Those where relatively minor injury is sustained

This broad category encompasses injuries which may or may not result in the victim being unable to continue the lesson, and may or may not require medical investigation/treatment. In many cases, these factors may be determined as much by the severity of the actual injuries as by their general nature, and common sense will be more valuable than a hard and fast set of rules. There are, however, several guidelines upon which an instructor can base responses to individual incidents.

a. Never make assumptions about a fall purely on the basis of sight and sound. A heavy fall may leave a rider virtually unscathed, whilst an apparently soft fall can sometimes have serious consequences.

b. Although it is a good principle to encourage a reasonably robust attitude in pupils, an instructor has a moral duty of care for them. He should not, therefore, allow/encourage any pupil to remount after a fall without first enquiring as to his well being.

c. It must be understood that it is not always possible for anyone other than the victim to evaluate the extent and effect of an injury (e.g. a pulled muscle), and indeed his own evaluation may not be entirely accurate. An instructor should, therefore, err on the side of caution, his general attitude being 'I don't want you to continue unless/until you are *sure* that you are all right to do so'. He should *not* encourage a pupil who is undecided about his physical well-being to remount, and he should certainly never badger anyone into doing so.

d. Even if a pupil claims that he is able to continue, an instructor should not permit this if he himself believes that the pupil's injury may significantly impair his safety and performance, or that continuing may aggravate the injury itself.

e. In addition to the possibility of a rider wishing to continue, whilst incapacitated, because of courage or bravado, there may be those who have been told (by other sources) that they will 'lose their nerve' if they do not remount immediately after a fall. Such foolishness is a very poor reason for a rider to pressurize himself into remounting whilst unfit, especially since there is the consequential risk of a further fall which *may* really damage his confidence. If a pupil should express such fears, he should be assured firstly, that the idea is largely mythical and secondly, that he will be given every assistance to remove any dents to his confidence he has recovered fully from any dents to his person.

f. People can sometimes exhibit significant shock reaction to falls, either without sustaining any real injury, or in association with the rather frightening sensation of being winded. Such people should not necessarily be written off for the remainder of the lesson just because they appear initially upset. Indeed, all other things being equal, they are the category most likely to benefit from being gently encouraged to continue once they have retained their composure. It should be noted, however, that nothing should be said or done which contradicts the principles in c) above. The approach should be along the lines of 'if you feel better later on, you might like to pop over a couple of small jumps'. This, in any case, is much more likely to earn a positive response than the 'come on, you're all right' attitude, which will merely provoke resentment and negativity.

g. Once it has been established that a pupil is fit to continue, he should still be given a couple of minutes on the flat before jumping. This is to *ensure* that he is all right. Some injuries – knocks, strains, etc. create a sensation of numbness rather than pain, and it may not be until he is riding that a pupil realizes the effect of an injury. During this period, therefore, the rider must be told 'if you don't feel ready, say so, and rest a while longer'.

h. Before a remounted rider takes another obstacle, it is sensible to draw to his attention any error on his part which contributed to the fall. Although this must be done with some tact, it must most certainly *be* done, in order that a repeat performance is avoided. This brings us to consideration of the third category of falls.

3. Those where no significant injury is sustained

Whenever a pupil suffers injury, an instructor's first concern must be with the injury. If a pupil is unhurt, however, the instructor can get straight on with the business of analysing and explaining the reasons for the fall.

Sometimes a rider may have a fall because his horse falls, or as a result of defective saddlery. When novice riders are under instruction these causes are (and should be) rare. If they *do* occur, the precise causes must be fully investigated, and every effort made to avoid any recurrence. The vast majority of novice rider falls are, however, of the rider only, and occur because balance is lost beyond the point of return. Such incidents may be the result of either error of technique or lack of forethought, and recurrence – if not the original fall – should be preventable by astute instruction. Although the horse's behaviour may be a contributory factor, no horse who makes active attempts to dislodge his rider should ever be employed for novice instruction. The instructor should, therefore, be careful that he does not readily lay the blame for a rider's fall at the horse's door – and neither should he encourage pupils to do so. For example, *excusing* the fall of a rider on the grounds that his horse refused or ran out ignores two fundamental points: firstly, the rider's role is to control the approach so that such events do not happen (if they do, he may possibly have engineered or provoked them) and secondly, even if they do happen this does not mean that the rider need necessarily fall off. Thus, while an instructor should never be harshly critical of a pupil who has just suffered the indignity of a fall, he must be entirely realistic in his appraisal of its causes, and prepared to draw the pupil's attention to any contributory error. Indeed, it will be apparent that any decent instructor has a fundamental *duty* to correct any error great enough to part a pupil from his mount.

Further to this, there is a question which all instructors should ask themselves in the event of a pupil falling: 'did they fall in spite of what I told them, or because of it?'

CHAPTER 12

INTRODUCING COURSES

THE ASPECTS of instruction already covered will familiarize pupils with many of the elements of jumping a course. However, to round off the programme of basic instruction, and draw these elements together, some time should be spent assessing and riding such courses as the instructor is able to devise. These courses should consist of obstacles and approaches of types previously tackled, the object being to introduce pupils to extended sequences of jumps, rather than to anything intrinsically new.

When introducing the prospect of riding courses, the instructor should emphasize the importance of course-walking for the purpose of establishing a detailed, decisive riding plan. He should, indeed, walk courses with his pupils, pointing out all significant factors. These will vary in detail from one course to another, but general points for explanation are:

1. It is helpful to know the general route of a course before starting to walk it, to avoid confusion and wasting time. It is always possible to establish the route of a showjumping course (as long as the fences are numbered) simply by looking; at cross-country competitions the course plan can be consulted and, if necessary, copied roughly.

2. The starting procedure for the relevant discipline should be explained. With showjumping, the importance of riding warm-up circles should be stressed. These must be on the appropriate rein, which is established by reference to the approach to the first fence and, in some cases, the route from the first to the second. Similarly, in cross-country, riders should be advised to keep their horses moving as much as possible prior to the start, and to ask for the appropriate canter lead rather than just dash through the start anyhow.

Course-walking: as pupils progress they should be taught the importance of measuring distances between fences.

Below: Studying and sketching courses plans will help riders in the battle of wits against the course-builder.

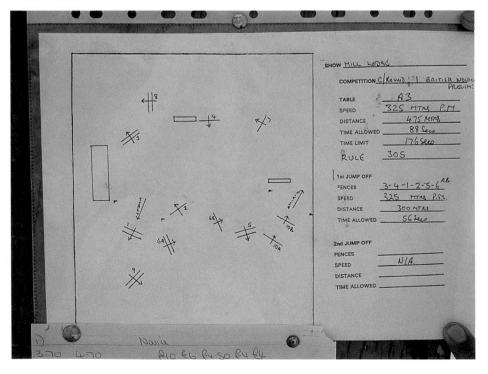

3. Throughout a course, a rider must determine the appropriate route and gait from fence to fence, bearing in mind the characteristics of each obstacle, the preferred line of approach, and actual or probable state of the ground. Changes of rein — and how to ride them — must be noted, together with any unusual/deceiving angles between fences.

4. A rider must not leave a fence until he has made a firm decision as to how he should jump it. In cases of difficulty, the best plan is to resolve to ride a strong, controlled approach along the most obvious line.

5. Striding must be checked in all combinations. Although novice riders will not be able to do this with the precision of experienced competitors, they should ascertain, at the very least, *how many* strides there are between elements. With multiple elements, it is worth checking whether distances are the same between each. It is also useful to know, in general terms, whether strides are short or long; where options exist, this may help establish the best line of approach. *Short bounce distances must be approached in trot.*

6. Where optional lines of approach exist, or if the line to a fence is rather obscure, it can be very helpful to note external features (trees, spires, pylons etc.) which can be used as guide points.

7. Anything on or around the course which may distract the horse should be noted. In addition to the attractions of the collecting ring, stables, horses/other livestock in adjacent fields, this may, at a show, include pretty well anything unfamiliar. A rider should be prepared to demand extra attention from his horse when in the vicinity of such distractions.

8. At the end of a course, riders must remember to go through the finish. This is not always as obvious as it may seem, especially to an inexperienced rider who may be elated just to have got this far.

9. Having finished a course, riders must ensure that they are in full control before leaving the course at trot or walk.

In conjunction with such advice, an instructor should explain the basic rules and penalties of the discipline concerned as appropriate. He should also, as necessary, point out the differences in rules and penalties between showjumping and horse trials. Similarly, when pupils are riding the courses, they should be made aware of any unwitting breaches which would be penalised in competition. This is important, since it can prevent the

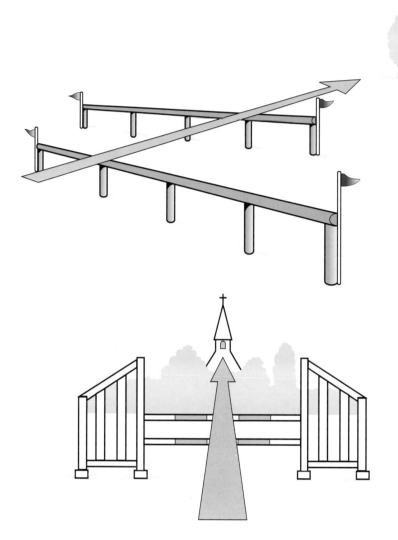

Using external features to establish lines of approach

disappointment of inexperienced riders whose first awareness of a rule results from innocent transgression at a show.

In other respects, while pupils are tackling a course, the instructor should not give advice unless they experience considerable difficulty. The object is for them to employ the skills they have already learnt, and to learn further independence. To this end, appraisal and discussion should take place after the course is completed, pupils being invited to assess their own performances first.

In Conclusion

A JUMPING instructor who understands his subject, and is prepared to apply himself wholeheartedly to teaching, has the capacity to expand greatly the range of equestrian activities his pupils can enjoy. In addition to the vocational satisfaction this should bring, it is likely to enhance his reputation considerably. It is suggested, therefore, that such a policy be pursued to the mutual benefit of both teachers and pupils.

ABRS ACCIDENT PROCEDURE

- When an accident occurs... **KEEP CALM AND KEEP CONTROL**

- Halt the ride in an orderly manner and in a safe place.

- Dismount and hand your horse over to a responsible person

- Delegate control procedures

- If on a road, post someone at each side of the accident to slow down and control traffic

- If there is a loose horse, send someone to catch it.

Go quietly to the injured person. If he is conscious, tell him to remain still. Ask if there is pain in any particular area. If there is pain or he cannot move fingers and/or toes on no account move him until skilled help arrives. Cover with a coat or blanket. On NO account give any liquid to drink. Stem obvious serious bleeding by applying light pressure to the wound with a clean piece of material made into a pad. Keep talking to reassure him.

If a person is unconscious, make sure there is no blockage in the mouth, watch the breathing carefully, cover with a coat, loosen clothing. Send for skilled help. Do NOT leave the casualty alone and continue to monitor breathing.

It is for the Instructor/Escort to sum up the situation quickly and efficiently. To assess the degree of injury. To know whether to allow the rider to remount and continue the ride or to send a message to the stables asking for transport to take the rider back if there has been a slight injury or to send very quickly for emergency service (999 call) to summon skilled help in the event of serious injury. On no account should a person be allowed to continue to ride if he/she has been unconscious – no matter how quickly the recovery may appear to be. Transport should be sent for, and the rider taken for a check up. Circumstances will dictate whether the ride continues or returns to base.

In the case of an injured horse, assessments have to be made to the same pattern. He may be able to be led back to the stables from another horse, or a box may have to be summoned and the vet alerted to be at the stables on the horse's arrival or veterinary assistance may have to be summoned to the scene of the accident.

In all cases, reassurance and a calm, workmanlike approach is very comforting, not only to the casualty but to the other riders as well.

On returning to the stables, make out a report in the Accident/Incident Book while everything is fresh in the mind. Take statements from other riders who were witnesses to the accident. The Insurance Company should be notified of any injury to a person, or damage to property, motor vehicle or the like which could result in a claim.